Also by Tammy L. Maté

Fame's Eternal Camping-Grounds: *A Historical AND the*
Original Authentic Accounts of the Civil War Battles
Fort Donelson, Shiloh, and Vicksburg

The Guerrilla Mystery: *A True Unsolved*
Mystery of the Civil War

SECOND LIEUTENANT GEORGE DODD CARRINGTON

Authentic Civil War Diary

The Companion to
Fame's Eternal Camping-Grounds

Introduction

by

Tammy L. Maté

Fame's Eternal Books, LLC
United States of America

For additional information, contact:
Fame's Eternal Books, LLC at
TammyMate@aol.com or
1-512-468-8873

CONTENTS

INTRODUCTION

I am privileged and honored to bring to you the authentic Civil War diary of my great-great-grandfather's comrade, Second Lieutenant George Dodd Carrington. The original diary, existing as scraps of paper and small tattered notebooks, is difficult to read. However, what you have in your hands today is what Lieutenant Carrington typed himself from his own pages. You will see that he later proofread his work and left correction markings.* It is a veritable miracle that this thoroughly detailed perspective of the Civil War exists today. Not only is it advantageous to have this firsthand documentation, but Lieutenant Carrington's writing style makes reading his day-to-day experiences entertaining and enlightening. The companion to *Fame's Eternal Camping-Grounds*, it is a must-read for anyone interested in the American Civil War.

Tammy L. Maté

*There were only 5 pages, which were so indecipherable that I felt obliged to type for you. These are pages 2, 77, 79, 80, and 81.

CARRINGTON BIO

Born in Litchfield, Connecticut August 10, 1842, George Dodd Carrington entered the world of iron foundry co-owner and foreman, Leonard Carrington, and his wife Ann Dodd, described by her grandson as a lady who wrote with "lovely emotional ability of expression."

Like many early Americans, George's family did not fear the abandonment of one's lifestyle for something altogether different and new—be it occupation or home location. George's paternal grandfather, John Carrington, emigrated from England to Connecticut, where he and his son Leonard jointly became owners of the iron foundry. In 1854, George's Uncle Edwin Carrington, who captained and co-owned a Mississippi steamboat, convinced John and Leonard to move their families to Camargo, Illinois to take up farming with him.

George's maternal grandfather—and namesake, George Dodd, was also a venerable man. Born April 5, 1778, he captained ships that sailed between the United States and Europe. It is recorded that in 1805, as he captained the ship *Vigilante*, slated for Bordeaux, France, the British at Portsmouth, England stopped him to inspect his ship for contraband. It was well publicized at that time that Bordeaux held frequent auctions of contraband items.

Besides his passion for adventure, George Dodd felt passionate about the importance of literacy. In letters to his daughter, Ann, he implored her to read every day. It is very likely, therefore, that Ann passed this insistence on reading to her son, George Dodd Carrington. In turn, once you have finished reading *Second Lieutenant George Dodd Carrington's Authentic Civil War Diary*, I think you will agree with me that Ann's son also had a gifted ability of written expression. Enjoy George's colorful, clear, and honest depiction of the western Civil War battles from his youthful perspective. Be the "fly on the wall" (or military tent) that you have always wanted to be.

Tammy L. Maté

at 22 years of age.

Front of postcard found in my great grandmother Leota Lyons's scrapbook.
Leota was the daughter of John Darnes Lyons, comrade to George Dodd Carrington
(and main character of *Fame's Eternal Camping-Grounds*).

Taken at Springfield Ills.

July 25th 1865

George D Carrington

2d Lieut. Co B.. 11th Ills Infty,

fathers old buddies in
_____ civil war

POSTCARD

Back of postcard found in Leota Lyons's scrapbook.

Photo on reverse is of George Dodd Carrington.

SECOND LIEUTENANT GEORGE DODD CARRINGTON:

AUTHENTIC CIVIL WAR DIARY

The Companion to

Fame's Eternal Camping-Grounds

1861

Lacon Marshall County Illinois.

April 22d 1861.   I enlisted in Captain Fred W Shaw's Company of

Volunteers for the three months service in defence of the Union.
We were boarded by the citizens until the 25th of April. We were drilled
in marching, meetings were held at the Court House, speeches were made,
songs sung. (Dixie seemed to be the most popular), merry making as if war
was a picnic.and so it then seemed. The only acquaintance I had in the
Company was Austin D Bragg, and David Stenger. Bragg not being well did
not go with us. Stenger was accepted and went with the Company.
The Company was made up in Lacon. Several joined from the surrounding
country, hence the name "Marshall Co Guards". Capt Shaw and a few others
were middle aged men, nearly all the rest were Boys from 17 to 22 years
of age. The number enlisted was 148. The Capt received word from the
authorities at Springfield, that he could take only 84 Privates, 4 Serg'ts
4 Corporals,2 Musicians, and 3 Commissioned Officers.
Making a total of 97 men. this number was selected from the 148.

The Company was organized as follows.

Capt Fred W Shaw.
1st Lieut Greenbury L Fort.
2d Lieut John McClanahan.

Sergeants.
1st Sergt Thomas Ellis.
2d "   Mervin Black.
3d "   Henry Burk.
4th "   Benj' F Blackstone.

Corporals.
1st "   Ralph L Tuttle.
2d "   George Wright.
3d "   Samuel Cutler.
4th "   Richard H Maxwell.

Musicians.
Isreal D Coburn.(Drummer).
Albert W Gore. (Fifer).

Privates.
1 Addington.William S.
2 Buck.Jerry M.
3 Boico.Welcome H.
4 Bauer. John.
5 Blanchard.Nathaniel.
6 Bender.James T,
7 Bommer. John,
8 Barnhart.Jacob,
9 Carmichal. Isaac.
10 Carrigan.John,
11 Carney.James F,
12 Carrington. George D,
13 Drake. Andrew,
14 Dean. Sam'l B,
15 Eisenhower.Casper,
16 Fox. Amos,
17 Fuller. John M,
18 Flemon. William,
19 Gay.George W,
20 Grey.Thomas,
21 Hatton. Andrew,
22 Hesse. Alexander,

Privates.
23 Hurlbut.Egbert R,
24 Hurlbut.Willis.
25 Hower. Solomon H,
26 Hall. Peter A,
27 Jenkins. Edwin,
28 Justice. Harvey,
29 Jones. Fred B,
30 Kuhl. Jacob,
31 Lewis. Thomas N
32 Liend. George
33 Larr. John W
34 Lynn. George
35 Laterette. Joseph
36 Leighton. Andrew J
37 Moren. Terence
38 Murray. Elijah J
39 Miller. John W
40 Morley. Howard C
41 Maurice.William G
42 Madden. James H
43 McDonald. Charles
44 Mc Donald.Arthur
45 Mc Kinzey. John
46 Mc Mahon. Daniel

(2)

Privates.

47 McAuley, Robert P	67 Traver, Jessee
48 Newport, Thomas J	68 Traver, Harvey W
49 Ogg, George G	69 Traver, August P
50 Piatt, James	70 Varney, Horace
51 Peck, Warren	71 V [?] twerp, Hiram
52 Powers, Alexander	72 Walker, Joseph
53 Rogers, Michael	73 Walker, Anderson
54 R [?], Charles	74 Wesley, James W
55 Rump, Harmon	75 Wise, Peter
56 Rump, August	76 Wiar, Solomon
57 Seabring, James M	77 Wilson, Cornelius
58 Sewall, Martin	78 Wimer, John M
59 Schell[?], Phillip	79 Wilcox, Alfred
60 Scott, Walter	80 Worley, Lorain A
61 Scott, Alonso	81 Wright, Calvin
62 Shaw, George B	82 Wright, Daniel W
63 Smith, John A	83 Wright, James W
64 Stenger, David	84 Zimmerman, Franc
65 Thompson, Henry B	85 Amos, Thomas #
66 Thompson, James	86 Lyons, John D #
	87 Sewards, William #
	88 Thompson, LaRoy #

Those marked with # joined the Company at Springfield and Birds Point During the Three Months Service.

Totals.

Com'sd Officers	3
Sergts	4
Corpls	4
Musicians	2
Privates	88
TOTAL	101

In the three months service, we were allowed only 4 Sergts. and 4 Corpls.
Two Musicians.

April 25th. The Company crossed the Illinois River, and took the train at Sparland for Springfield. We rode on down having a fine time, cheering as we passed the people along the road. They swinging hats and hankerchiefs and cheering back at us. War is popular, or is it just a picnic

April 26th. Arrived at Springfield. Left the train and marched out to the Fair grounds called Camp Yates.
Impressions at the Gate.
We were without arms or equipments of any kind. In citizens clothes of all kinds and colors. Some carrying carpet sacks, others bundles of clothing. I had nothing but the suit I was then wearing. And as we marched through the gates I shall never forget the sights that met our gaze. The impressions of that moment. It was night and very dark. At the gate on either side were sentries armed with musket----

(3)

--and bayonet, There was probably 10,ooo men in the Camp.Standing around
the camp fires, with red three point Mackinac blankets over their
shoulders,The darkness, the glare of the camp fires, The red blanketed
men passing to and fro, The cattle pens, high board fences, Other building
with the glimmer of an occasional bayonet; All made up a scene never to
be forgotten; Especially by Boys just from home where nothing war like
was to be seen, We were alloted our share of cattle pens for quarters,
and issued a red blanket each, Wrapped in these we lay down on some straw
that had been mercifully provided for our first nights sleep in camp.

April 27th

Rain and mud, Besides we have to cook out of doors,We were provided
with an iron pan called a mess pan, Rightly named if one could see
the messes" that were stewed in these pans,A camp kettle also of
iron, A frying pan, tin plates,and tin cups, Somebody,the Government

I guess furnished us with bakers bread, fresh beef, beans and coffee
The beef steak was fried until it cupped up like an old saddle
skirt, the coffee was boiled until strong enough to "bear up an
iron wedge",and black as a hat,(This fare made many of us sick,
and many never fully recovered from eating of this awful cooking)
But we learned to cook fast,(And afterwards could set a table with
rations that was both palatable and wholesome,) but suppose we have
to get used to this.

April 28th,
                Sunday,, Weather pleasant, In camp and drilling, Boys in
good spirits and full of fun.

April 29th, I sleep with my clothes on ,generally take off my shoes,
                roll up in the blanket and nestle down in the straw,
                        nights not very cold, But this sizzling of frying pans,
                the smoke and smell of cooking, Whoopee",

April 30th, Fry beef and burn it, beans not cooked half enough, black
                strong coffee with out milk, The bread will do,My stomach
                is out of all regulation with such out-landish grub,

The Capt brought 84 Privates to this camp, But was notified that 64
would be all he could retain, There fore 16 men were cut off (two had all
already gone home,),Myself among the number dropped,I then along with
the only friend I had in the Company,Went over. and joined another-----

(4)

-company called the Union Tigers, Our quarters were up in an old
stable loft,We were soon tired of the Tigers,And joined another
company, While in this Company was detailed for guard duty, was
given an old Harpers Ferry musket and bayonet,Some kind of a Corporal
marched us out and stationed the guards along a high board fence,
out side the grounds with orders to let no one in or out. After the
Corpl left us we stood our muskets up against the fence and enjoyed
our selves jumping and at the same time watching for the Corpl,
Who would find us all on duty, after being here two hours the relief came and we returned to quarters, After dinner word came that Capt
Shaw had received orders to fill his Company to 84 Privates,
Upon hearing this we stole out our red blankets the only property we
had and went back to Shaws Company.I was off duty four hours, So
when the guard was called I watched them form; Trembling, while I
"peeked through the cracks in our quarters.My name was called but
I did not answer, however some one took my place. I was afraid of
being arrested, but no notice was taken of my delinquency,
I saw the guards march away and breathed easier, Consequently I
played off first time I was ever called upon to do duty.,

May 1st, The drilling and organizing goes on, as well as the cooking,

May 2d, I have no money or I could buy some"grub"that would agree with
    my taste a little better,

May 3d, We were sworn into the U,S, Service for three months(to day.)
    A carriage drove in through the gates and seated alone was
    Stephen A.Douglas, bare headed and bowing right and left as he
    was being driven around the Camp and out at the gate,For the
    Boys took after the carriage on the run,and shouted, yelled,and
hurrahed for Douglas in a perfect stampede.Knowing He would be
overwhelmed by the enthusiasm of the Boys he was driven around and
out without stopping, I never saw him afterwards.

May 4th,

Marched down town to day and received a musket, bayonet, and
cartridge box,with a shoulder belt,these with our red blankets
constitute our entire Government equipment, We were now organized
as Company "B of the Eleventh Ills Inftry, Col W H L, Wallace
commanding, Iooo strong,Have been drilling two or three times each
day, and we keep the step pretty well for green soldiers,

May 5th,

How proud I was as we marched down through the streets of Spring--
-field at 4 P M, to take the train , with the drums and fifes
playing the "Girl I left behind me", We were formed in column of
platoons and kept the step fairly well,with bright muskets, frying
pans, camp kettles,and red blankets tied over our shoulders

The flag we so proudly bore, our hearts swelling with soldierly
pride and patriotism,Reached the Depot aboard the train and on d
down the Central, Cheered all along the way,We shouted until hoarse
to the men,women, and children who waved their hats, handkerchiefs,
and seemed full of enthusiam, It is all hurrah; Boys so far.

May 6th, We arrived at Villa Ridge, A small town on the Central. got off
the cars marched out a short distance to Camp,They had prepared for
us Popular board buildings, Each Company had rooms facing a parade
ground, Am on guard at the cars to night.

May 7th, Went up to camp this morning after being relieved from guard do
duty, to find scargely any thing to eat, found some fat pork
and a cracker,placed on a chip of which I made my breakfast.
Some thoughtful comrade saved a portion for me even small, I
growled some, a soldiers privilege.

May 8th, Our camp is named Camp Hardin, A quarter of a mile east of
Villa Ridge, We occupy quarters as follows, Barracks made of
pop lar boards,each building has a partition through the center,
So that each Company has half of two facing the street or parade
ground between,There are bunks in three rows one above another,
Back of the quarters are large beech, gum, and poplar trees and
affording shade, Several fine springs of water under these trees
furnish our water supply,Officers, and Head Quarters as usual in
such camps, King has a sutler store on the extreme right, Near the
center of camp is a large, tall hickory flag staff,—

(6)

with a bunch of branches and leaves untrimed at the top, Ground is
sloping sufficient to carry off the water and drainage complete,
We have a fine parade ground large enough for the whole Regt' to
march and drill. Squad, Company and Battalion drill with guard ,
picket, and fatugue duty keeps us busy,There is a good deal of "left"
"left",going on in camp . Am not very well,
Capt Coats is our drill master and comes about every day for an hour
or so, drills us in the manuel of arms, We like to have him show
us how to handle a musket he is so plain, and trys to teach us the
principals, Scotts Manuel, The shoulder or carry,arms, is the piece,
with left hand under the butt plate erect at the left shoulder"
barrel to the front, all the movements are from this position.

May 9th, Adjutant Hotchkiss is a very fleshy little man, In dressing up
          the Regt' for drill or parade rushes up and down the line
puffing and perspireing carrying his sword extended well in front,
Some times slips its point under the buttons of a mans coat as he
passes along, So he would have to back out and move on again with
a pleasant "excuse me","dress up there", "dress up", "your toofull".
and no wonder just after eating a hearty dinner of beans,
He would finally get the lines at ppen order, all straightened out,
"Arms at an order, Parade rest,Band on the right consisting of ten
drummers, ten fifers, and a huge bass drum would lead off and play
down in front of the line and back.Then present arms and the Col
gives a few orders in the manual of arms. Reports by the Adjutant, D
Dismissal, First Sergt's take charge of the companies, Back to quart

May loth, There are lo Companies in the Regt' lettered from "A to K"
          inclusive,"A"is the first on the right, we are the second, then
the others on down to "K." Our muskets are 69 calibre, " turnip
slingers" we call them, altered over from flint lock to percussion,
Use paper cartridges,"(pronounced cat'ridge") short,(a round ball
and three buck shot,) When dishharged nearly knock a man down, mine
is not so bad as some, If we could hit a barn at loo yards it would
be a happen so, It requires no skill, The original flint locks would
be better as we could pull the trigger and dodge before the explosion
would take place,

Nights, after the drills for the day are done,

May 11th

Company "A"s quarters   getting

the Boys to form in by placing our hands on the front mans shoulders
in single file
one after another, Winding in and out of the Companies quarters,

keeping step as we are so close cant help but step as the man in front

of you steps, until we have five or six hundred man marching around

like a huge snake. Then we go on up to the Col's Head Quarters,

and call him out for a speech. After winding up in a solid ball ,

a great mass of men, with cheers , and hurrahs. We then listen to all

that is said, then break up and off to quarters. So there is some fun

mixed so far with our camp life,

We drill Scotts Tactics. The formation is in two ranks in line, right

face and march in two ranks by the flank, The manual of arms is .

The musket at the left shoulder, The left hand supporting the piece

at the butt plate, piece erect, barrel to the front, This is Scotts

carry, From this the support, the present, and the charge, No finer

movement in the manual. At the command "charge bayonet", Grasp the

piece at the small of the stock with the right hand, Carry it around

to the right side dropping it smartly in the left hand at the lower

band, at the same time carry the right foot three inches to the rear,

making a right half face, knees slightly bent, point of the bayonet

hight of the eye.

Our cook shanties are made by setting four forks, one at each corner.

then lay on some poles and brush, making a shelter from the sun but

not much good in rain storms, Drive some stakes in the ground, nail

some cross pieces, then fasten a couple of boards on top, and we have

a table, one board for seats the same, Two pieces of rail road iron

layed on a brick at each end make a fire place to cook on quite

convenient and handy,   plates, cups.

knives and forks, as well as other cooking utensils, while in camp.

On the march each one carries his own out fit,

May 12th, Sunday. Rain and mud, rather rough on the boys that have to
            stand guard.

May 13th,
            The first death from sickness in camp, about day light I
        heard the most dismal and to me , doleful sounds, The shrieking
        of fifes playing the dead march, accompanied by muffled drums,
        as a squad of six men with their muskets doubled under the coffin
        carried the body to the train to send home.

May 14th,
            Some sickness in camp, mostly camp dysentery. some fever,
        nothing very serious, the change in food and water causes
        stomach trouble. Our cooks are improveing,

May 15th,
            We are yet wearing our citizens clothes and getting rather
        ragged, Few of us have any money to buy· any thing with, hardly
        scare up enough to buy a postage stamp.

May 16th.
            Private Jones, is a tall, lank, jolly sort of a fellow.He
        wears a pair of blue overalls, these reach down abbut four inches
        above his shoe tops,He has a way of hauling them up about half
        way to his knees, and in shirt sleeves, with an old straw hat firmly
        planted on his head, He would then grasp a musket with both hands,
        the piece in a horbzontal position, and march up and down the
        parade ground giving the command, "Left",Left",at the same time
        bringing down his left number ten shoe with great energy, also
        the musket,The sight is very comical and we boys enjoy it hugely.
May 17th,
            It seems to me the most severe strain on our nervous
        system is after eating a hearty meal to stand in ranks and hold
        a musket at carry arms in the hot sun for ten or fifteen minutes at a
        stretch, We looked forward to the manual of arms drill each day
        with much interest, As we learn fast and prefer it to marching.

May 18th, We received our uniforms, consisting of a grey coat fitting
            down to the waist, then a short frill or skirt, with light blue
        trimings and brass buttons, grey pants, a blue cap. one pair socks
        one pair shoes, and one shirt,The new clothes were badly needed

-as ours were badly worn,and some wore getting quite ragged,
We are getting the hang of the drill and think we are pretty smart
soldiers by this time.Make a fine appearance on dress parade,

   Genl Prentiss visited our camp . We received Him with cheers while
      the Band played "High Daddy in the Morning",

May 21st,
         We formed on the parade ground in line, From line we passed by
         the right of Companies to the rear onto column,then marched in
         review before Genl Prentiss, making a very creditable appearance
         Visiting citizens viewed the parade,
         (The Lithograph on first page was taken at this time),

May 23d, Col Wallace left Camp last night,
May 25th, The drilling goes on , camp duties&c,

May 26th,   Tom Lewis and Terrence Moran went down to the spring back
            of camp and had a fight, What it was about I dont know,

May 30th, We are not getting any money, but King gives us credit at the
          sutler store for any extras we think we need, and he waits
          until pay day,

June 1st, One the sick list, Target practice but I did not go out.

 June 3d, Raining, Some better to day,

June 5th, I lie in the top bunk while sick, this is also My sleeping
          place, the Boys in the night, keep up a racket, calling like
          birds and cats, barking like dogs and all kinds of sounds
          they imitate, Dan Wright sings "Bound all around with a woolin'
          string", over and over, so they keep it up half the night,

June 10th. I take my medicine and lay around, getting some better,

   June 17th,
            The usual amount of drilling, guard duty, and fatigue duty,
         going on all the time, Fatigue duty means work other than
         drilling or guard duty, such as (policing) cleaning up around
            camp, loading rations,&c &c,

-- Company going out for target shooting. Am not able for duty,
   but am able for rations just now,(did not go with them,)
   Afternoon, The Regt returned from target practice. Boys with black
   eyes, bloody noses, black spots on faces and shoulders. Old muskets
   kick like a mule, nearly knock a man down. Some of the Boys are
   afraid to shoot. Mine does not kick so bad.

June 18th, Boys go out in the country and buy corn bread for a change.
   I noticed Peck coming in with both hands full.

June 19th, Pretty hot down here in "Egypt," as they call this country.

June 20th, All packed up ~~and~~ to leave Camp Hardin at 10 A M. Got aboard the
   cars and made the run down to Cairo 12 miles. Left the cars, went
   aboard the Boat and crossed the river,(The Ohio and Mississipi
   come together here,) over to Birds Point Mo. Pitched our tents
   about dark and at last got a place to sleep,(Sick all night,)

June 21st, Better this morning. Harvest time here. There is a small
   breast work here enclosing about one Regt' of Inftry, two six
   pounders and one 24 pounder mounted on the works. Suppose there
   will be other Regts' here shortly. Fired on a Boat over at Cairo
   and made her land.

June 22d, Sunday, All quiet about camp. Last night a little after dark
   Companies "A" and "B" of our Regt'(The 11th) with several Companies
   from Cairo ~~went~~ went aboard the Steamer "City of Alton" and
   steamed up the river to surprise a "Secession Camp." Being too sick
   to march I remained on camp.

June 23d, Weather warm. No news from the boys. Our camp is on level
   ground back a short distance from the river. A large dwelling
   house where Mr. Bird used to live, is now used as a hospital,
   for sick soldiers. Farther back is low land and a solid mass of
   heavy timber, The Mississipi river flows past on its way south. The
   Ohio comes in from the north east and being clear water mixes with
   the muddy water of the Mississipi forming patches of clear and muddy
water until far below it is of one color, muddy, We use the river water
for drinking and cooking, pretty thick but there is none other,.

(11)
June 26th, Boys returned to camp, when they reached the "secesh" camping
place the birds had flown, After some hard marching in the heat they
returned and such a blistered up "set" I never saw before. We have shoulder
belts for the cartridge box, waist belts for bayonet scabbard and cap
box, where these belts, crossed and around the body were broad bands of
red blisters, foot sore and weary, many of them could scarcely wear shoes
or shirt for a week or more, very few complained, thinking all this the
natural order of military life, Last night a company of artillery
came in from the north with four six pdr guns, we have now seven pieces
all together, "Bully for us," Moved camp inside of the breastworks,
busy setting up tents &c, Our rations are soft bread, fresh beef, beans,
coffee, tea, sugar, rice, soap, salt and candles, good enough for any body
if we can only get the cooking done right, but we are learning quite fast,
Small baker's started up near the river, where we can buy pies and such
things, that add nothing to our general health in the long run.
June 27th, A boat came down the Mississippi and not blowing her whistle
at the blank signal gun fired from Fort Defiance, Cairo, was fired at
again with a solid shot, causing her to blow her whistle and land at
Cairo, Thats $5.00 out of the Captains pocket for not answering
the first shot. clear and warm.

June 28th, About sick this morning, Afternoon , Fired on a steamer,
the ball went whistling on its way and struck the water on the Cairo
side of the Boat, throwing up the "suds" full ten feet, Fort Defiance,
is some with her long 32s,

June 30th, Weather hot, Last night there was a musket fired , out on the
guard line, the drums beat to arms, And in about five minutes the Regt
was formed in line of battle, A false alarm ,A day or so ago the 18th
Regt, Ills, caught and drummed out of camp a secessionest. He swore
revenge, so about 9 p m, a man supposed to be the same "old coon" sprang
upon one of our guards, with a pistol, the guard struck the pistol to
one side, it went off doing no harm, the guard then fired his musket,
it also missed its aim, the other man then drew a bowie knife cut the
guards arm, the next sentinel coming up at this time, the man ran off and
got clear, hence the alarm. after finding out what the matter was we
went back to bed. where we remained until,
July 1st, about three oclock this morning, muskets and cannon aroused
us from our sleep, we were soon under arms and in line, ready for a fight,
But this also proved to be a false alarm so we retired to rest once
more, it was raining most of the time and very dark, so much so that
I could scarcely see my file leader when marching, we discharged our
muskets into the river and at an old Ferry boat for our morning salute,
Afternoon nothing stirring, all quiet, weather warm, Some talk of the
three months men being paid off,
   July 2d,
         Last night saw the comet for the first time, it was in the
North West and towards morning was very beautiful, cool and chilly this
morning, Working on the rail road, the rise having caved the banks in
we were obliged to move the rails in order to save them.
July 3d, Weather pleasant, preparing for the 4th, The River is rising
fast, banks are caving in, The current full of drift wood, logs, chips,
and whole trees, the body of a man passed going on down stream, The
boys went out in a skiff but could not bring it to land, having been
in the water so long that it was bloated and partly decayed, therefore
they let it go on,
July 4 th,
         Last night another alarm, the report of a musket out on the
guard line, this would alarm the camp," Fall in "after a great deal of
bustle and excitement, boys couldent find their shoes: " where's my
cap"? got cartridge box on upside down, every thing mixed up. but these
tangles gradually came out all right, grab a musket and get in ranks,
we marched out in double quick time, but it proved false and resulted
in the death of one hog," on the picket line", At sun rise the big 32s
at Cairo are blazing away, also our six ponnders here at the Point,
making quite a noise, Balloon ascension at 12, (noon) A very small one
and soon out of sight. The great question that has been raging in our
Company, in regard to reenlisting for three years is settled at last,
thirteen members of the Co "B", for three years, the rest bound for
Lacon Ills, when our time is out.

July 5th,

All quiet in camp, Battalion drill at 3 p m ,Hot,but we have to
stand it as Soldiers,
July 6th, Commenced work on the new breast works, the old ones are
washing in the river, weather hot,
July 7th

Recd'a letter from Lacon Ills,   Traded some coffee for black
berries, the first for the season,and very nice ones too,
hot as usual.
July 8th, I went over to Cairo,to day, had a good look at Fort Prentiss
(as it is now called), Saw a 64 Pdr on the cars the largest gun I ever
have seen so far, there are three 32s, and three 24s, one six Pdr brass
piece used for hailing boats, and one mortar in the fort,the large guns
are on frames and pivots so as to command the Ohio and Missipi in all
directions ,

July 9th, Last night I was on picket guard east of camp, about twenty
of us under command of a Lieut, we marched out in the woods,,brush
tangled vines,.weeds,and grass, here we sat down in a group ,had to keep
awake all night no relief,there in the sultry night air, mosquitoes
the droning of bugs and other insects to torment us, we would drift off
in drowsy,almost asleep,only to have the Lieut. grab us by the shoulder
"wake up there",Had I been depending on myself I could keep awake, but
I was letting the Officers do the depending.All these alarms and night
watches, amounted to nothing,   the whole camp was alarmed and a good
deal of firing toward the Depot and up the river from us,No one hurt,
we saw nothing unusal on our post, Towards morning a storm arose and
blew nearly all our tents down, besides filling every thing with dust,
Day light we returned to camp this being my first picket adventure.
The Capt with the three years men started for home to day at 4 p m ,
on a furlough of ten days, as soon as they return think we will be
discharged.

July 12th, Weather hot for last three days, nothing stirring,
Am on guard, 9 a m The steamer City of Alton came down bringing the
22d Regt of Ills Infty, three Regts here now,
July 13th, Relieved from guard duty this morning and returned to camp.
at 1o,A,m,a company of cavalry 64 in number arrived on the Str David Tatum,
July 14th, Sunday, weather clear and warm,Received one shirt, and one
  pair of drawers , from Uncle Sam, Am much better in health to day than
for some days past.I hear of one case of cholera in camp.
 e have since learned that our men killed three of the enemy and badly
wounded a forth, on the night of the 8th, July.
July 15th,

We were routed out twice last night "on alarme",but as usual
proved false, I believe they are only trying us, Had a"bully"dinner of
corn beef soup and sour bread,- some rain to day,

July 16th, Cleaning up the Camp, looking for the Capt and his men ,
Some talk of us going home this week . Am not very well to day,

July 17th, The Captain arrived this morning early, with 3o men ,
  Austin D Bragg, , enlisted and came with them, My old comrade.
They came before breakfast so we had to give them some thing to eat,
which we did.

July 18th, Last night I had to work unloading a flat boat, we took off
about nine or ten cords of wood and quit for the night.
The gunners in Fort Prentiss are practising,they fired several shells
some of them burst in the air,and others struck the water, bounding like
  rubber balls,in the night they look like rockets,

July 19th, Cool and pleasant this morning,Had pancakes for breakfast,
One of Company "A,"s men was drowned while in the river bathing,
searched all day for the body but could not find it, the swift current
carried him down the river,

July 2oth,Cool this morning, Picked a cotton blossom the first one I ever
saw, A man buried to day he belonged to the 18th Regt,

July 21st, Sunday, cloudy, Inspection of arms and equipments by the Col.

(No 12)

July 21st.

     We drew what they called a"Havelock".A white cotton cap cover
with a flap or skirt to hang down and coverthe back of the neck
as a protection from the sun. The hottest things ever worn.Keep all the
air out and leave one to swelter with the heat. We soon settled these
things by making dish rags of them. We do not like the large black hats
worn by the new Regiments,but prefer caps, as we think them more military
These caps are made so the circular top instead of drooping forward stand
straight up. An Irish Boy in our Company called his a"Whicker bill"
with the accent on the bill" So that is the name adopted.

Two men were drummed out of camp for some misconduct. There was a file
of men with bayonets pointing to the rear, then another file of bayonets
at a charge. Between the files of bayonets marched the two men while
the fifes and drums played the rogues march.
"Poor old Soldier; Poor old Soldier; Tarred and feathered and sent to
----

----

hell" because he would'nt Soldier well".

One of them seemed very much ashamed and hung his head. While the other
held his head up and marched erect,bold and defiant.

(I never saw any one drummed out of camp after this . We had better
use for men).

(13)
July 22d, All wet and mud the"dell " to pay generally,heavy thunder
storm, most of the messes in their tents were drowned out, and sometents
blown down, rained hard all last night,   got breakfast finally, had
about two good cakes to the man, well it will not pay to grumble,we are
Uncle Samuels Soldiers. Afternoon, sun shines t'will soon be dry.

July 25th, Still in camp and waiting, three months to day since we left
Lacon,and a long time it seems to me, weather hot'.

July 28th,,Sunday,cool and pleasant this a m, Was on guard duty last
night,guarding the cars on the Fulton and Cairo rail road,slept in the
cab of the engine, there were three of us and we took it by turns two
hours each.
July 29th, Relieved this morning at 9A, M, The steamer Des Moines,
came down to day, they hailed her at Cape Giradeau and the boat not
stopping fired into her with muskets, and reported killed five men,
The boat came by camp with her flag at half mast,12 more of Capt. Shaw's
men sworn in for three years.

July 30th, Mustered out of service,The Company formed in line. those to
remain step two paces to the front,the rest of us standing with arms at
a support, as our names were called brought our muskets to a carry then
to order and so mustered out of service, no discharges were given for
the three months service, dismissed and to our tents,
I purchesd a picture of our Camp Hardin,when Genl Prentiss was there
and we marchedin review,   (see front page),(Company reorganized),
                                              (July 30th,1861)
   July 31st, Well?we are mustered out but not paid yet,I cooked breakfast
this morning, had Slapjacks! meat and coffee, after breakfast washed a
pair of pants at the river.
(This is the end of the three months service.)
August 1st, Birds Point Mo, Sick and hot,

Aug 2d, Great rejoicing in camp, The Steamer City of Alton, first,with
Genl Fremont on board, next Steamers Louisana, A D January.G W Graham,
War Eagle, Warsaw, and Jennie Deans, with about five Regts aboard
came down the river from St Louis. Saw Genl Fremont, The 17 th Ills
is on board with Company"B " No 2 from Lacon,

Aug 3d Genl Prentiss, said this morning We would get our pay to day,
   about ten men sun struck, fearful hot.
Paid $58,65 for the three months service.(in gold and silver)

Aug 4th Been up to the Hospital taking care of one of my mess mates
who is sick,   a man died here just now,A man was was accidently
shot on picket last night, by one of his comrades, buried to day.
I intend to continue as a member of Co "B", and remain in the service.
but am going home first and stay as long as I wish, then for the three
year service.

(14)
August 5th, Left the Point took a boat over to Cairo, Got aboard of the
cars and started for Lacon Ills. we arrived at Centralia, here the train
stopped, I got off to find something to eat, I met a woman who said she
was sorry for the sick boys, I asked her where I could find some thing
to eat," come with me " so we started on the run up an alley, she making
 pretty good time and myself close behind, soon turned in to an open door
in the kitchen, table set, she snatched up pieces of chicken, grabbed
bread, pieces of cake and pie, (handed to me for I was in a hurry not
knowing how long the train would wait)" saying "My heart bleeds for you
poor boys", however, it was quite comical to see Me chasing a woman up
the alley, of course she was taking the shortest way to her kitchen.
I thanked her for her kindness and sympathy, and hurried back to the train
both hands full, I divided with the other boys who like myself were about
half sick. After a hot dusty trip arrived in Lacon,

Aug 7th, Arrived at John Stuarts house 4 miles south of Lacon,
  Found all friends well, and glad to see me. blackberries were ripe,
so I ate blackberries often, thinking they would be of benefit ,
I remained here untill the ,

Aug 19th, Left Lacon and arrived at Tuscola four miles from My Fathers
house, walked this distance, and arrived home, on the 22d of August,
Remained at home resting and visiting until.

Sept 2d, Left home, took the train for Birds Point Mo.To rejoin my Regt,
I had to go back to Decatur as my pass was on the main line of the
Central R R, Father took the train on the branch, after getting aboard
found Maj Ransom of the 11th, had I known he was aboard ,he would have
passed me through as I was one of his boys, However I went around and in
 due time arrived at Cairo, crossed over the river and once more in camp,
Father had reached there before Me, and had found quarters in the Capt's
tent,

Sept 5th, Arrived in camp at Birds Point Mo, Father met me as I was coming
up the river bank from the boat, found the Boys alliright,

Sept 6th , Sworn in to the service, for three years as drummer, of Co "B"
11th Ills Infty.

the Company is organized as follows, For the three years service,

Company as reorganized on July 30th 1861, at Birds Point Mo.
Company # B" 11th Ills Infty.

Capt Fred W,Shaw,
First Lieut Alfred R Wilcox,
Sec'd   "   Samuel B Dean,
Sergts,
1st Sergt Warren Peck,
2d   "   John W Larr,
3d   "   George B Shaw,
4th   "   Charles A Blackman,
5th   "   LeRoy Thompson,

Corpls,
 1st Corpl Elias T Coleman,
2d   "   Thomas C Edland,
3d   "   Enoch J Cunningham,
4th   "   John Morris,
5th   "   David Stenger,
6th   "   Thaddeus S Young,
7th   "   Thomas Amos,
8th   "   Andrew Drake,

Later,Musicians
   George D Cabrington, # Drummer)
   John J Stuart, # Fifer)

Privates,
1 Austin Sales,
2 Bragg Austin D,
3 Bennington William J,
4 Barnhart Jacob,
5 Coffee John,
6 Collins John,
7 Cummings Stephen W,
8 Connells Henry,
9 Crayton Alfred,
10 Crane Charles W,
11 Coan Daniel W,
12 Egan Francis,
13 Fred Phillip,
14 Green William J,
15 Groves Jacob W,
16 Greenleaf Leonidas,
17 Hall PeterA,
18 Heater Francis M,
19 Hesse Alexander,
20 Lyons John D,
21 Lewis Thomas N,
22 Linscoft John S,
23 Linscott Anthony,
24 Lorch Alexander,
25 Lockner John G,
26 Larkins Thomas B,
27 Madden James H,
28 Morris William,
29 M'Cure William,
30 McMahon Daniel,
31 Murray John B
32 Newport Thomas J,
33 Onager Jacob,
34 Plummer William,
35 Powers Alexander,
36 Perry James K,#
37 Powers John H,
38 Phelan James W, #
39 Rump August,
40 Roberts Johnston F,#
41 Ross James,
42 Sewards William,
43 Shanklin Joseph A,
44 Springer Daved,
45 Shaw Worcester O,
46 Smilie Marshal,
47 Terry Peter G, #
48 Vaugn John,

Privates,

49 Vernay James D,
50 Vore Isaac D,
51 Wagoner Jermiah,
52 Whitfield Alfred,
53 Walker Joseph,
54 Wright Daniel W,
55 Arnold Joseph,,#
56 Justice Harvey;p.#
57 Kunsman Phillip.#

Total
   Commishond Officers 3
Non "   "   " & "   " 13
     Musicians,   2
     Privates,   57
      Total,   ----
                        75

(Those marked # enlisted later,)

In the three years service we are
allowed 5 Sergts, and 8 Corpls,

Sept 7th, Went up the Rail Road to guard a bridge, Had a good time,

Sept 8th, Sunday, We are yet at the bridge.

Sept 9th, Returned to camp. Father left for home, The 2d Iowa Regt came
in to day, There is two Regts on the Kentucky shore this evening,
The 28th Ills and the 23d Ind came down the river on the Alex
Scott,The 8th Ills has gone out in the country for a fight I
guess, Four of our Companies have gone out scouting, It is now about
time for tatoo,

Sept 10th,Very warm to day, Nothing much going on, No dress parade on
account of four Companies being absent,

Sept 11th, Raining, Every thing quiet about camp, Camp Holt on the Kentucky
shore has four Regts, The 17th, 19th.24th.Ills and the 7th Mo.
One Company of artillery, and three 32s, mounted,Cloudy and damp,

Sept 12th, The 20th Ills came in just now, No letters from home yet,

Sept 13th, All well and quiet, The drum corps practicing,

Sept 14th, Tom Amos is the bully of the Company,A big chested short
heavy set man, They say he is a mountaineer, Some of the boys
are afraid of him, Others dont care to have any trouble with
him,He'll take a slice of beef steak lay it on the coals and
as soon as it cups up will eat it with the juce running down
between his fingers,Takes his blanket and sleeps out on the weeds.
When he gets a little whisky in him he's a bad man, When Jim
Phelan a tall Irishman came to the Company he disputed the
supremacy of Amos, as the Company Bully, They were rather shy of
each other, There must have been some trouble between them, For
later on Amos deserted,We heard of him being in the artillery in the
Rebel service,How true this report was we never knew, Phelan also
deserted while we were at the Point,and before the(Donelson
Campaign) Such men never make good soldiers.

Sept 15th, Pleasant and cool. Not well to day. No news from the boys at
Norfolk as yet. All quiet about camp.

Sept 19th, Our old Drum Major(Mc Qullion) came to day,now the drummers
will have to practice and drill,

Sept 20th. Weather pleasant,Wrote letters home, Did some washing,

..... 21st. .... whiskev.He's an
get over to Cairo

Our loss at the Battle of Ft Donelson. Tenny
Feb 15th, 1862,

```
1   Capt Fred W Shaw,          Killed.
2   Private,Joe Walker,         "    "

3   1st Lieut A R. Wilcox,     Wounded. (Died of wounds.)
4   John Vaughn. ,Private,      "    "    "    "  "    "

5   2d Lieut S B. Dean,         "    "
6   1st Sergt J D Vernay,       "    "  (Taken Prisoner),(right arm)
7   Private J S Linsott.        "    "   "   "  "    "
    "     " D McMahon,          "    "   "   "  "    "
8   2d Sergt J W Larr,          "    "
9   4th Sergt C A Blackburn,    "    "
10  1st Corpl E T Coleman,      "    "
11  5th Corpl D Stenger,        "    "  (Col Corpl),(both arms and leg,)
12  Privates.
12  Barnhart Jacob,             "    "
13  Coffee John,                "    "  (Arm & Side),
14  Crane C W,                  "    "
15  Eagan Francis,              "    "  (Eleven Wounds),
16  Green Wm J,                 "    "  (In thumb)
17  Hesse Alexander,            "    "  (Through shoulder),
18  Linscott Anthony,           "    "
19  Larkins T B,                "    "
20  Murray J B,                 "    "  (Slightly)
21  Plummer William,            "    "
22  Powers John H,              "    "
23  Peck Warren,                "    "   (Slightly,Buck shot),
24  Springer David,             "    "   (  "    "  )
25  Whitfield Alfred,           "    "  (Leg & hand),
26  James H Madden,             "    "  (Slightly)
27  George D Carrington, ✓      "    "   "    "
```

--guard duty or fatigues He has a way of saying " Whin the bullets do be
   flv'n where'll yer extra juty min be thin",

Sept 22d,We marched down to Norfolk on a visit to four of our Companies
         that are already there, we had a good time eating Pawpaws on the
      way down, We left there ,the Drum Corps playing the " Girl I left
      behind me",and reached camp about 6 P M, Came in playing "Yankee
      Doodle"

Sept 23d, Left Camp Lyons this afternoon and arrived safe in Norfolk,
         I am sitting on my drum writing by a nice fire of secesh rails,

Sept 24th, Cool and pleasant, Feeling pretty well,Suppose we will stay here
         to day at least, Made a visit to Norfolk.The 22d are quartered
         here also the 8th Ills. The 2d Iowa just went north, The 7th
         Iowa is on the steamer Louisanna, Ready for a march from all I
         can learn, We will have a fight there being plenty of secesh
         around,

Sept 25th, Left Norfolk at 1030 A M, and arrived in Camp Lyons about noon,
         It seems like going home to get back to Birds Point, Boys are
         in fine spirits,

Sept 26th. Rained last night, cool this morning, There is to be preaching
         to day, Afternoon. Our Chaplin preached a fine sermon under an
         apple tree, The whole Regt turned out besides some others,
         After the sermon the Band played the"Gal I left behind me".
         Then we returned to our quarters.

Sept 28th, Cool this morning makes the boys draw near to the fire, This
         evening we were honored by a visit from Genl Grant, The Regt
         marched in review before Him,

Sept 29th,   Sunday, There is to be an inspection of arms and equipments,
         Which came off this morning, This evening there was a man buried,
         He belonged to the 2d Iowa,Regt Co" C.It was a solemn thing to
         see the Company march without arms.The Band playing a very slow
         time, The coffin borne by six men, Two files of soldiers with
         their muskets reversed, They fired three volleys over his grave
         , May he rest in peace. Bragg has been sick in the Hospital,
         Feeling some better came over to see me and visit with the Boys,
      As I was cooking I had him stay and have dinner with us, The beef
      steak tasted so good after being on Hospital diet that He overdid--

---himself and ate too much, Going back to the Hospital very sick and came
      near dying, I can't see how it is we are always hungry, This camp
      dysentery seems to keep a man hankering for some thing he ought not
      to eat, Its the water that effects Me most, This river water has so
      much sand in it, One can get all the " sand in his craw" he wants
      and not half try,

Oct 1st,   To day we turned over our wedge tents and drew new ones,Nice
      large round tents called the Fremont tent,They will accomodate
      16 men, Have a center pole with arms extended some thing like an
      umbrella, in the top so we can hang up our haversacks and other
      things, We sleep in a circle around the pole.
            The 7th Iowa just came in also the 8th and 22d Regt'sIlls.
            One Company of artillery.

Oct 2d,   This morning at one oclock we were awakened and ordered to pack
      up for a march that the rebels were in Charleston, So we
      marched up to the cars got aboard and rode about four miles, Then
      Left the cars and took it afoot by this time the rain poured
      down, reached Charleston , but did not see any thing of the
      rebels,Rested and ate our dinner, Then we marched about two or
                                        laid
       three miles south of town and layed in a corn field about four
      hours, No enemy to fight , took a few prisoners then turned
      back marched to the rabl road got aboard the cars and returned
      to camp tired ,hungry, wet and all mud, I rode in on the tender
      as the cars were crowded,

Oct 3d, In Camp Lyons , Manage to clean up and get dry once more,

Oct 4th Out at Charleston Three Regts of Inftry and Taylors Battery

Of Artillery, One company of Horse and a long train of wagons,

We got up early packed up and with two days grub in our
haversacks started for the cars, It was dark and looked like

rain, aboard the cars and rode about four miles , then we
got out in the woods to take it afoot, By this time the rain

was pouring down, The roads very muddy, day light began to
appear ,We started on resting once in a while until we came
to Charlston where we expected to find a large force of the
rebels, But the "bird had flown" We then camped on a level

place , cooked our dinner, got what little rest we could.

Then started on a south course and marched about two miles
till we came into a lane with corn fields on both sides,
Here we halted the supOsition being the enemy were close at

hand, One 12 pounder gun was placed at the head of the lane

We got over in the corn and waited about four hours with out
seeing any thing of them , Then we marched back to Charleston
All we saw in this town was negros and small fry , old men

and women, We took some prisoners , good many of the Boys gave
out.that is about all it amounted to, I stood the trip first

rate carried my knapsack, two blankets, drum, oil cloth,
haversack, canteen, all wet and mud, coming out of Charleston

We played the "Gal I left behind me". Charleston is quite a

pretty place , has two churches , some large brick buildings
fine trees &c, It is built on a small prairie, Most of the

houses arevacated, and there is an air of desolation about
every thing. Saw the place where Col Ransom had his fight

also where he was wounded, One of the Churches has a good

many bullet holes through it , We were all sure of having

a fight when we started but were badly disappointed, I heard

an officer say that there was yor 600 of the enemy in the
country some where but we could not find them,
Took the cars and landed at the Point about 9 P M, Broke
ranks and got into quarters as best we could all wet and mud,
We came straggling in after dark through the rain amd mud,

Boys firing of their muskets towards the river, rather than

to draw the loads after getting into camp,This alarmed the

troops over at Cairo,

(In the early ,5os My Father was a member of a militia

   Company in Conn, The Boys used to call the three commission

   Officers . The "Forward Captain,"Middle Captain". and Hind

   Captain",)
Thats about the way we straggled into camp, In squads,
groups, with Captains and without Captains, But we got there
all the same,

Oct 5th, The usual camp duties,

Oct 6th, Sunday, Wet and muddy, Last night it rained so hard there was
six or seven inches of water in our tent had to scatter around to
find a place to sleep, This morning went to work and dug ditches
around the out side, filling in with soil, the inside so now I
think we wont get drowned out the next time it rains.
Reported New Orleans taken,

Oct 7th, This morning about 2 oclock we pulled up our stakes rolled up
the tents and about sun rise piled on the cars   for Charleston
where we arrived all safe , Our Company going out on a scout,
No enemy in sight yet, There is two Regts and one Company of
artillery with three 6 pounders and one 12 pdr gun pointing towards
the town, One Company of horsemen. There is no body here but darkeys
and children, A little after dark a man was shot through the
shoulder by one of the guards,
About the first thing after breaking ranks the boys ran for a
large orchard close by, the trees loaded down with apples, The Second
Colonel soon put a stop to that by putting a guard around it,
Then the owner sold apples 6 for 5 cents, There is also a tobacco
house near, full of the weed, The boys nearly robbed that,
One of my mess mates' went out and brought in some sweet potatos,
Said he "drawed them," by the tops of course, When one asks "where
did you get it, "I cramped it", That is he took hold of the article,
his hands "cramped" so could not let go.

Oct 8th,   Quietly in camp, One of the boys was out after dark and returned
with some "contraband" sweet potatos,"

Oct 9th, Charleston Mo, well we are yet in camp a little out of town,
Have had no fighting, I hear we will go back to the point,
Pleasant weather now with cool nights makes a fire feel good,
especially in the evening. Left Charleston about 10 o'clock,
Arrived at the Point and camp late in the day, We rode 8 miles and
footed it about 4, miles,

Oct 10th, This evening one of our men ran and jumped in the river and
drowned himself, He had been sick in the Hospital for some time.

Oct 11th, Drew new hats, We dont like them , They are grey with the
sides turned up so they can be buttoned to the crown on each
side, with a kind of a beak in front, Austrian Hats they call them,
The Regimental Brass Band came to day,

Oct 12th, Fine weather, All quiet,

Oct 13th, Sunday, A very pleasant morning , Puts one in mind of a Sunday
morning at home,,With the Church bells ringing, Our quarters
are clean and every thing looks nice and pleasant, We have no
duty to day except such as is necessary,

Oct 14th, Nolmans Cavalry had a fight south of here in a corn field,
One was killed ,three wounded. and four horses wounded, there
was about 150 of the enemy against only about 30 Of our men,
they succeeded in escaping after a pretty hard fight.

Oct 15th   All quiet in camp, usual drills, parade &c,

Oct 16th, Had a grand review to day, Six Regt.s of Inftry, One of
Cavalry, and a battery of artillery. Several men buried,
We played for a funeral.One of the Cavalry men that was shot
in a fight down by Norfolk. was shot in the head lived two
days then he died and we gave him a soldiers burial,
We drew blue overcoats nice long ones with capes,for winter.

Oct 17th, Feel pretty well this morning, Cloudy like rain. Our Company
gone to the bridge, all quiet about camp,

Oct 18th Company returned from the guard,

Oct 20th Sunday, quiet.

Oct 22d, Frost this morning, One recruit joined the Company,
One of the boys shot his forecfinger off, accidentally.
I find a drum is a hard thing to carry, It is always in the
way, either by my side or on my back,

(22)B

Nov 6th, No word from the boys yet,

        All packed up for a start, Where I do not know, going at 4 P M,

        All the men on the Point, Took the cars for Charleston,

        Arrived about 8 30 P M, Stayed all night,

Nov 7th. Left Charleston,
We started this morning and marched through the sand nearly
ankle deep. The day was warm, I marched in the ranks having loaned my
drum to one of Co I" Boys,Carried musket and cartridge box with 40
rounds, We marched 28 miles and Camped for the night at a place called
Hunters Farm, Here the Boys killed goats, sheep,hogs and chickens,
Had all we wanted to eat, We are under Command of Col Oglesby,
He having started two days ahead of our Division,They went to Bloomfield,
And we met them 7 miles the other side of that place, we then marched
together to Cape Girardeau,There was nearly 100 wagons and 5 Regts of
Inftry, two pieces of artillery, Also a long line of Cavalry,We were after
Jeff Thompson but did not catch him, (Then ordered back to the Point on
account of our defeat at Belmont)
Myself and four others gotin advance of the Column aboutthree or four
miles, So we could stop at houses and buy corn bread, One place there
was a little boy came out and asked me for a hard cracker, I gave him
one, He said he would get some apples, So we gave him all the hard bread
we had,He went in the house and brought out a pan full of apples,One of
the Boys gave him 15 cents, The people along the road said they had not
seen wheat bread for two or three months,We stopped at one place,a large
house, A great many dogs and darkeys around, We asked for corn bread,
Apparently the Owner told one of the blacks to bring us some, She went
in the house and soon came out with a plate full, also about two quarts
of butter milk, We ate the bread and drank the milk, thanked them and
started on our way,As we were anxious to keep ahead of the Column,
Arrived about 3 Oclock at our camping place,The rest of the train did not
come up before sun down, So we had a good rest,

Nov 8th, Had a tiresome march through the swamps, There is growing here
a black curly moss, which the boys called the "Nigger wool swamp
Camped for the night on a small stream, The Castro river it is
named, clear water, We are tired and foot sore.

Nov9th, Started early this morning and came up with the boys about 10
o'clock, Greeted them with loud cheers, We are about six miles
from Bloomfield, Camped near some mud holes for the night,

Nov 1oth, Marched all day , and reached Duttletown about sun down and
        camped for the night, having marched about 25 miles. We are
        now 9 miles from Cape Giraideau.

Nov 11th, On the way early , Arrived at the Cape about noon, quite a nice
        little town. There is a Fort on the hill commanding the river
        and the country around. The Ladies presented our Regt' with a
        wreath to put on the flag, camped for the night,

Nov 12th, Embarked on the steamer Alex Scott for Birds Point, Where we
        arrived safe at sun down, And are again settled in our quarters,

Nov 13th, Weather pleasant, cool and all hands in good spirits,

Nov 14th, To day we turned over the old Harpers Ferry muskets and were
        furnished with French rifles, calabre 69 same as the old ones.
        However with these we use a conical bullet. ounce and a 1/4 in
        weight,paper cat'ridges,large percussion caps. Waist belt for
        bayonet scabbard and cap box, Canteen and haversack, knapsack to
        strap over the shoulder to carry clothing&c, Two large grey
        blankets per man, This is a Privates out fit, A pretty good
        load while on the march,

Nov 15th, Damp and cloudy, Our Company going out to the Bridge, All quiet
        about Camp,

Nov 17th, Sunday, Rain and wet, Last night a couple of our boys had an
        argument, quarrelled.and ended in a fight.

Nov 18th, Had a grand review of our Brigade before Genl Grant, A long line,
        First the 8th Ills. 1oth Iowa, and 22d Ills, Then came the
        Cavalry, Next the 11th Ills, 2oth, Ills and 7th Iowa, Then
        following Taylors Battery, made a fine appearance, the 1oth Iowa
        lost a good many men at Belmont so their line was not as long
        as usual,A deserter came in our camp from Columbus, went over
        to Cairo to report. Says there is 25000 men in Columbus,

Nov 19th, This morning we started about 2 o'clock, Left camp went aboard
        the cars for Charleston, Jeff Thompson passed through about 8
        o'clock last evening, We started at 9 this morning in pursuit,
        Drove in his pickets but he escaped as usual,

--He had just robbed the Steamer Platte Valley, Brought her too
with a couple of pieces of artillery, 6 pdr's, Then " skeddadled"
taking his guns with him, We halted about 9 miles from Charleston for
dinner, Marched back reaching there about dark. The cars being in
waiting got aboard and returned to the Point, Set in raining so we
got all wet through,Each one went to quarters as best he could,
water ankle deep all over the camp ground,

Nov 20th, Sun shining, mud drying,

Nov 21st, Pay Master here, paid off, received $ 24.00 two months pay,
Pleasant and drying, all quiet about camp,

Nov 22d, On duty as Orderly at Head Quarters, Take orders from the Colonel
to the different Company Commanders,&c,

Nov 23d, Moved our tents, Getting ready for winter, Letter from Father,

Nov 24th, Sunday,All hustle and confusion putting up cabins for winter
quarters, Seems wrong on the sabbath day,

Nov 25th, Cold, ground frozen this morning, All hands busy building barracks
log cabins going up all around us, Went over to Cairo, 4 Companies
of the 20th Ills left on the steamer Memphis, She has 6 or 8
holes through her chimneys received at Belmont,

Nov 28th, Cloudy, rain and mud, One of our men reported deserted,
Barracks going on slowly,

Nov 30th, Snowed last night, cold, Sun shines this morning, wet and muddy,

Drum Corps had to play for funeral this morning before breakfast,

Dec 1st, Sunday, Working on the barracks as usual, Buried a man of the 8th
Ills, One of the rebel gunboats came up the river just now and
sent three shells into Fort Holt on the opposite side of the
river, The Fort returned the compliment with about four or five
rounds, They sent two shells from the Fort in Cairo with what
damage I do not know,   The rebels are getting quite saucy,One
of our artillery men stood on the bank and fired his revolver at
the gunboat, They returned the fire by sending over two shells
one burst near and the other brought into camp,

(26)

Dec 26, Cold, Snowing, All hands at work on the Barracks.

Dec 4th, Pleasant this morning, work on the cabins as usual as we are in
           a hurry to occupy warmer quarters, Some are cutting out doors
           and windows, Others making fire places.

Dec 7th, Last night about 12 to 1500 Cavalry men went out after Jeff
           Thompson, Some where near Belmont. More rain,

Dec 8th, Weather pleasant enough to work on the buildings,

Dec 9th, On duty as Orderly at Head quarters, Carrying messages to
           Officers, Reports &c, Letter from Sister,
           We beat the reveille at 6 o'clock in the morning,(Early these
           cold mornings) Sick call at 7 A M, Guard mount at 8 A M,
           Practice at 10 A M, Play for Battalion Drill at 2 P M, Dress
           Parade at 6 P M, Tattoo at 8 o'closk in the evening, Taps at
           8 30 P M, Lights out.,go to bed,
           On account of so much work on the Barracks, Afternoon drill and dress
           parade are ommbtted, Taps ends the routine of the day while in
           Camp,The Sick call,"Come git yer quinine" quinine", come git
           yer quinine" Lots of it used here,

Dec14th Last five days about the same as usual, Elected W Wright, As our
           fife Major, Mc Quillon is our Drum Major, (He was in the Mexican
           War) Wrote a letter to J J Stuart, Who was our Company fifer,
           Sick and gone home,Hammering away at the Barracks!,

Dec 16th, Had an inspection and review, The 11th. Was pronounced the
           best drilled Regiment at the Point, Just before we started Col
           Wallace says "Now boys if ever you did march do it now",
           And we did,

Dec 21st, Moved into our"shantys" all right for the winter now,,Well fed
           and comfortable, On one side three bunks one above the other,
           At the end a fire place, I am cooking for the five Sergts.they
           pay me $1. each per month,My pay as a drummer is $12. per month
           theirs is $ 17. making mine equal to theirs, First Sergt Peck is
           my bunk mate, The other Sergt's are Larr,Shaw, Blackman,and
           Tompson,

Dec 22d Sunday, Rain and mud, just got in our quarters in the right time,
           Sunday night, Boys all singing, happy and contented in our---

---new cabins, We have a pleasant fire in the fire place. Dark and wet
        out side,

Dec 23d, About a 1000 of the Cavalry started for Belmont,

 Dec 24th, Christmas Eve,

 Dec 25th, Our Capt gave four chickens to the mess, We are going to have
        two for dinner, and keep the others for tomorrow,
        (Merry Christmus( ), all,

 Dec 26th, Boys are cleaning up quarters, Weather wet. Parade ground
        muddy. Wrote letters home,

 Dec 28th. Two of our pickets taken prisoner. Two darkeys" came away
        from New Madrid, Making use of them, One is cooking for the
        Capt, The other works around for the Boys, making rations at
        least, At night the boys have them singing and dancing, lots of
        fun in these "darkeys,
        Our duties continue the same, drilling, guard duty, fatigue,
        inspection,My drumming and cooking keeps me busy, from 5.30
        A M, until 9 P M,

Dec29th, All quiet, The log cabins are fine for winter quarters, We set by
        by the fire in the fire place of evenings and are very
        comfortable and cosy,)

 Dec 3oth, We have to get out early to beat the reveille , wake the

        Boys up for roll call and breakfast, then sick call." Cant git
        "e'm up. cant git 'em up" They come a running some with their
        shoes in their hands, others putting on pants and coats as
        they come, Any way so they get in line and answer "Here"to
        their names as they are called,

 Dec 31st, Muster for pay, The last day of the year.
        New Years Eve,
                        1861

1862

Jany 1st, 1862,   *1862*

        There is a great deal of camp talk about our leaving this

Camp Lyons, Birds: Point Mo. Reported we leave to morrow.

        As I did not like the regulation drum I bought one that suited

me better and paid $ 8. for it, The old one I sent to my Brother

at home, It is a good one but needs some repairs, made of pine staves

and shell of birds eye maple and does'nt hold up in the wet.

        We are having a muddy time of it now, The river is rising fast

nearly over Fort Holt on the Kentucky shore,

        Oysters and crackers for dinner, Made molasses candy in a camp

kettle, (about half full),

    Boys having lots of fun, turned their coats wrong side out and called

them selves "Jeff Thompsons Cavalry", They rode about camp at a

break nack speed, Several were run over and one man got kicked

in the head,

Jany 2d, Some measles in camp, After the yellow jaundice, and what next,

Jany 3d Talk of leaving our warm cabins, They seem so home like but

guess we can stand it,If we have to,

Jany 4th, If we leave dont know wether will go up the river or down,

      (weigh 165#)

Jany 5th, Camp quiet usual duties.

Jany 6th, Paid two months pay to day $24,

      The Regt marches in two ranks when marching by the flank,

Some times strung out half a mile or more,

Jan 7th.   After dinner we have orders to march with 24 hour rations,In

about half hour were on the way,Marched down to Norfolk. did not

see any "secesh, So we marched back to camp and arrived about 4 P M

No one suffered unless it was the"grub",After supper we sat talking

about going to bed, When the Capt opened the door,Told us to be

ready by 8 P M,with 24 hour rations, (this was delightful),We were

going out to capture a rebel camp some 3 or 4 miles from Charleston,

We started from camp went aboard the cars and rode 11 miles then we

left the train, landed in the woods and about 1 oclock or a little

after, Took it a foot around through the woods,(I believe our guide

must have been a "secesh,"for he kept us going about all night)

Dark and raining, We musicians marched at the head of the column

carring our drums all wet, and ourselves drenched through, One of the

Officers rode a white horse and we just could see the outlines of

this particular horse, So we plunged along through the rain and mud,

The 10th Iowa Inftry were just ahead of us, The 20th Ills and some

Cavalry in all about 2500 men, We managed to follow in the pitch
                    about 5 A M,
black darkness, Finally towards morning while we were marching XXY
through a lane with corn fields on each side and a house with a

blurr of trees ahead, There rang out on the morning air the clear

sharp report of a rifle,followed by a flash of fire and the

reports of a volley of musketry, The Iowa Boys returned the fire

We halted,some confusion, only tempory for Col Ransom sang out

" 11th forward on double quick", and soon had the Regt in line,

And we drummers to the rear, We moved forward in the darkness, MM

but the enemy knew the woods and " skedadled", No more shots
were fired, We remained quietly until day light,(Well We smelled
gun powder)",some 4 or 5 of the 10th Iowa were killed and 5

or 6 wounded, the wounded were cared for best that could be done

then,as I came along a little boy says" I am wounded, where?

why on the head says he, He fell down and hit his head on a rail

poor fellow,I looked at the men killed lying there dead with
the rain beating down on their faces it did look so hard,
We felt much depressed at the sight of those poor fellows lying
there dead alongside the road all wet and uniforms all
splashed with mud, --- We learned several of the bush whackers

had been at a dance in the house near by, hearing of our approach

lay in the woods, Having their horses tied back in the brush,

Intending to fire into our advance then mount and ride away,
Which they did succesfully none of them being hit by our bullets
The Officers ordered the man at the house turn out with his team and haul
the wounded under cover, -----

Jan 7th------Not finding any more of the rebels we marched back and found

        the cars waiting for us, climed aboard and soon returned to

        Camp Lyons at the Point,

    Note #,

        (In 1868, I harvested in a field with a man who was in this
         squad of guorrillas", Was at the dance, Told how they fired
        into the head of our column then got away on their horses)

Jany 8th, Yet in our cabins.

Jany 9th, No movement as yet, The fog is so thick Boats can not run,

        Some two or three are fast on the bar, Think we will not

        get off to night, If we go down it will be to Columbus and

        if we go up the river will go to Paducah, Very little snow
        but abundance of rain and mud. Our Company lacks about 40

        men of being full, It will make no difference all that are

        able will go,,

Jany 10th, Our mess is well except the cook has a bad cold,

Jany 11th, As the measles are going around I might as well have my

        share, It lays me up for a few days,

Jany 12th, As I lay up in my bunk sick with the measles the Boys made

        some hot whiskey toddy" and gave me several doses, Not bad

        to take,

Jany 13th,   Getting better,

Jany 14th, The Regt left Camp went aboard the Boat and off up the

        river some where, Not being able to go left me in the cabin

        to take care of equipments &c,

Jany 15th, Quiet in quarters, Am getting along all right ,much better,

Jany 16th, No news from the Regt, quietly in camp,

Jan 17th,   Getting over the measles,

Jan 18th   Several of the boys are down and others convalescing,

Jan 19th. Weather bad for marching, so much rain and mud,

Jan 2oth. Regt returned, They were down in Kentucky, marched some 8 or

        1o miles of Columbus but did not attack that place as most of

        them expected , had a hard march through the mud, but returned

        all right, they were gone about a week, no fighting and all were

        glad to get back to the old quarters,

Jan 21st, Weather cold the river is full of floating ice and rising very

        fast, Boats run as usual, Orders on the march ,There is to be

        no plundering, Some of the 22d Regt Ills ,Boys stole some honey,

        Genl Grant said he should have one dollar taken off each mans

        monthly pay, And $5, off all the commissioned Officers,for one

        month, As they were marching along ,"some one would sing out,

        "Who stole honey, Answer,"Genl Grants body guard","Who paid for

        it,"22d Regt Boys,

Jan 22d, For rations we have coffee and sugar, Tea if you buy it your
        self, some times they issue tea, rice, vinegar, potatoes, h

        hominy, beans , beef and pork salted.soap and candles.
        salt and pepper, and for change we draw at times sweet

        potatoes.apples,chickens, fresh beef and fresh hog,
        On the march we boil a chunk of salt pork, this sliced down
      cold to eat with hard tack is fine,

Jan 23d,The guard house is about full of secesh prisoners.

Jan24th. Captain Shaw gave orders to dispose of all surplus clothing,
        as we expect soon to leave the Point,we are to retain only

        what we can carry conviently in pur knapsacks, we drew a
        new uniform of blue to day, leave off the grey now,
        Dark blue jacket, light blue pants,and cap of dark blue.
         I sent home two coats, one pair of fatigue pants one cap
        and one blanket. Our new out fit will cost $6,75 cheap,

        but these are gov prices,
        I now have on hands.,one blanket, one oil cloth, one overcoat
        one dress coat two pair pants. two caps, one hat, one pr shoes
        one pr boots, three pr socks, four wollen shirts, three
        fatigue shirts. besides haversack, canteen, knapsack, and
        drum, enough for one man to carry,

Jan 25th, I received a letter from Sam Ford of the 21st Ills. ————

(32)

-----camped at Ironton Mo. He states a good many of the Boys are

"getting married for three years or during the war"

Jan 25th, The river is high and rising,They are building a stone wall
on the outside of the Fort over at Cairo,

Jan 26th, I think some of going into the ranks, as private's pay is

$ 13, per month,and musibion only $12, besides a musket
is easier to carry than a drum.

Jan 27th, All quiet about camp,

Jan 28th, Camp is in pretty good health now, the Boys that had the

jaunders looked rather yellow for a time, I had a touch
of it but the Docters"black stuff" knocked ot out of me
in a hurry, it was awful to take,

Jan 29th,   Charley Crane is the "yellowest Boy in the Company.

Jan 30th, ,   Some of the boys are providing them selves with

Boots for this muddy and wet weather,

I like the Dovernment shoe the best ,
Jan 31st,
Muster for pay as it is the last day of the month.

Feb 1st,
We are yet in our cabins but expect soon to leave,

Feb 2d,   Preparing to get ready for some kind of a trip.
Whoever occupies our cabins after we leave will find them
very pleasant to dwell in,

Feb 3d, We finally left our comfortable quarterswent aboard the steamer
A D January at 3 o'clock this morning, Most of the Regt found
quarters in the hold, The boys have candles stuck along on the sides
of the hull to light up the dark place, They are quite warm and
comfortable, Our Company and others were placed in the cabin,Large
cakes of ice are floating in the river, The weather is very cold,
Camp equipage, rations, artillery and horses on this Boat,

--Backed out and after stopping some time at Cairo steamed on up the

Ohio river and landed at Paducah about 8 P M, Took on three Parroit

guns, placed them on the forward deck, Later I lay down for sleep;

Feb 4th, Some time in the   night left the landing and steamed on up

the Ohio. When I awoke this morning we are up the Tennessee

river, Tied up and taking on wood, There is some 13 or 14 Boats

loaded with soldiers on this expidition, Where we are going do not

know, Left the wood yard and on up the river, Landed about four

miles below Fort Henry, Left the Boat marched out a half mile or so

from the river on the bottom land, here we bivouac, Back the bluffs

rise rocky with brush and timber,

Feb 5th,   This morning we moved camp near half mile father inland,

We are without tents or shelter of any kind. Have our overcoats

and two large grey blankets per man   man, During the day some

heavy firping from the Gun boats shehlling the Fort, The big guns

at the Fort returning the fire, Capt Carson the Scout just came in

bringing a rifl , sword, and a secesh flag he had captured, One of

Col Dickeys' Cavalrymen killed in a skirmish, As night came on a

cold pelting rain set in and kept it up nearly all night,

                  an
We are in bivouac in awopen field on a side hill, There is plenty of

rails and wood for fires, Laid a platform of rails in the mud to

sleep on, Lying on these rails as fast as one side soaked through,

turn the other side toward the fire, All this dreary miserable

night we suffered from cold and wet , Wool blankets are but little

protection from rain.
        (
(Rubber blankets were unknown at this time, I shall never forget
      that awful night,of cold and rain)
And thus we steamed ,soaked and shivered all this dreadful night,

Coming right out of warm cozy quarters, this night of weather horrors

gave many a stout young man his death warrant,(But we kept our

amunition dry),The dismal hours of night wore away and morning

dawned at last,

Feb 6th,   This morning the weather cleared up, The boys twisted and wrung

out their blankets getting most of the water out of both over-

coats and clothing, Prepared breakfast as best we could then

ordered to march. Which we did , through mud and water some

times four feet deep,----

---When we started this morning it was intended for the Inftry and artillery
to cut off the enemies retreat on Ft Donelson. Before we reached the
road they had left.Leaving a field piece or two stuck in the mud,
However we kept on and at 12 o'clock the Gun Boats opened fire and
advanced up the river towards Fort Henry,In hearing of those awful guns.
part of the time out of sight as we marched along over the hills,At
times could see the Fort through the smoke, The Boys would cheer when
the heavy reports echoed among the bluffs, Supposing it was the Gun
Boat guns, But we after-wards learned it was the big rifle in the Fort.
After one hour and fifteen minutes of heavy firing the Fort ran up the
white flag and surrendered, As the Inftry all escaped only a few
artillery men that maned the guns were taken prisoner,
After the firing we soon reached the Fort or rather the ground back of
the Fort, Here we stacked arms and after breaking ranks the Boys broke
for the Barracks to see what we could find, In one cabin they had been
baking bread a pan was on the fire and two or three cakes lying on the
hearth just as they had left, they seemed to be in a hurry, We found
rifles, shot guns. knives and some grey uniforms,Yellow seems to be their
favorite color, A big bass drum in one cabin, I picked up a letter dated
Oct 17th 1861. Directed to Thomas P Hutchens, It seemed he belonged to a
Company called the "Yellow Jackets" from Mississipi, On the back of this
letter I wrote to Father,
The ditches around Ft Henry are full of water and very deep,At the
entrance is a draw bridge, Many a poor fellow would have lost his life
in trying to take it by storm,In the Fort five men were killed , four
by the bursting of the big rifle, they got a shell fast some way and
the gun burst, The face of one man laid up on the gun, some eight or
ten feet of the muzzle rested on the embrasure, while the breech was
blown into fragments some of the pieces weighing 500 pounds or more,
were scattered around, One of the men had his head and both arms blown off,
A red flanel shirt partly around his neck.These five men are a fearful
sight. There is in the Fort 17 heavy seige guns, one burst,, One lo inch
gun that carried a 128 pound ball, These lo inch round solid shot seemed
to roll over the gun boats like rubber balls, One gun was struck in the
muzzle and dismounted, The fire from the gun boats was terrific, I dont
see how men could work those guns under such a terrible destructive fire,
The parapets and embrasures were torn in great rents where the shells had
gone ---

(35)

-----through scattering death and destruction all around, The log cabins
are back of the Fort, Shells had plowed their way through the logs
from one cabin to another, No wonder the enemy left.The river being near
bank full gave the gun Boats the advantage of being almost on a level
with the Fort and cabins.After the Gun Boats started and opened fire
they never stopped but kept right on up the river and landed at the Fort
taking the surrender from Genl Tilman,The 18 th Regt got in a little
ahead of us,

Feb 7th, It would take thousands of men to man these breast works and
rifle pits, The barracks or log cabins much like those we left
at Birds Point would accomodate quite a large number.
But they are all gone and we are in full posession, They fell back
on Ft Donelson, We captured several tents, The one we occupy is
marked " Nelson Greys", It comes very handy to shelter the Yankees"
as the "Greys have "Skedaddled", Several prisoners and horses were
brought in to camp this afternoon, Our camp is about half mile
from the river on a side hill. Our Cavalry got after the retreating
rebels and captured the brass guns they left in the mud,and a few
prisoners also, Reported several dead bodys were found buried in
the Fort,

Feb 8th, Raining and chilly this morning, Just got through breakfast of
coffee, hard bread, and some "secesh'corn beef, very good, They
estimate that a good deal of valuable material has fallen into our
hands,

Feb 9th, Pleasant clear and cold, Remain in camp, Our scouts just came
in bringing a secesh flag, 23 prisoners with some horses,
Our Orderly had a sabre given him, captured by the scouts,

Feb 10th, Quietly in camp, getting ready for a move,

Feb 11th, Left camp at Fort Henry about 4 o'clock this afternoon,As we
marched out on the road the Drum Corps at the head of the Regt
we played several tunes, As Fort Donelson is only 12 miles
away the rebels could hear us coming, Moved on about 4 miles
then in an old field we bivouac for the night, Made up fires of
dry rails. Living by the fire writing these notes, Was Orderly
to day, The 11th Regt leads on this road,

Feb 12th.
Up this morning , and marched all day, Skirmishing going on
in front, The 29th Regt lost three killed and four wounded,
We marched here and there and finally came in sight of the Fort
on a hill.A long line of rifle pits and breast works,from the Fort clear
around to. and beyond the little town of Dover on the Cumberland river,
The road from Fort Henry is up hill and down through the woods. Occasiona
-lly a clearing, There is some firing as the different Regts are getting
into position, We bivouaced for the night in a ravine as a shelter from
the rebel fire, While marching to reach this position some of the
advance Regts fired into another Regt by mistake in the darkness,however
we got settled for the night there is plenty of wood for fires and dry
leaves for bedding,

Feb 13th,This morning managed to get some thing to eat in the shape of
coffee and hard tack,Went down to a small creek filled my canteen.
From here I can see the tents inside of the breastworks, Three
secesh flags flying on their works.Our men are firing at the rebels

as a man exposes himself once in a while. The bullets are whizzing
over our heads from their side,Our lines are formed along the crest
of a ridge facing nearly north,The first Brigade to the right,
reaching down near the Cumberland river, Our Regt the right of the
2d Brigade, Taylor's Battery to our left and Swartz Battery to the
right farther down in the woods."Details have been digging out pits
just under the slope of the hills to plant our guns, Some artillery
firing, Shells and solid shot are flying over and falling far to the
rear, There is some old logs and brush piles near the top of the
ridge, From this shelter the Boys are firing at most any object on
the opposite side, The trees have been cut down with the tops out-
ward so as to make a tangled thicket almost impossible to get through
Small jack oaks slashed,with heavy timber to the rear, It does'ant

seem very far from the ridge we occupy across to their lines.
We have the same position selected the first night we reached here.
Night coming on I crawled under a burr oak bush that had dead leaves
on the branches,With dry leaves for a bed wrapped in my blanket I
laved down for sleep. Some time in the night was aroused by the order

--to " fall in", I was warm and very comfortable, Throwing off my blanket
I found snow had fallen to the depth of four inches, The chill night
air set me to shivering with the cold, The boys got into line,
bullets were whidtling over our heads,It seems the pickets have been
driven in but the enemy fallen back, They want to keep us awake,
Must be about as hard on them out there in the snow as for us,
The boys built up fires down in the lowest part of the ravine and
gathered around to get a little warmth. Leaving their muskets in
line by sticking the bayonet in the ground , A whole row of muskets
standing there ready to be grabbed at a moments notice, Firing would
again bring them into line,I made some coffee and sat by the fire
the rest of the night. We are some thing like," Napoleons shivering
Battalions in that blinding snow storm at Eylau,"

Feb 14th,Snow and cold, Sharp shooters are firing , Balls whizzing past

even now as I write these notes,The 17th Regt in a charge yesterday
lost a good many men, were repulsed.This morning snow on the ground
blankets frozen,Several of the boys hit with spent balls during the
day, At 4 P M, The Gun Boats ppened on the water batteries, After
some heavy firing they were repulsed and fell back down the river,
We could hear the rebels cheer; sounded like small boys, School boys,
yelling, The Gun Boats had been so successful at Fort Henry that we
were rather gloomy at their being repulsed, The rebel guns are
planted in pens dug out on the side hill close down th the river,
And it is almost impossible to get a shot or shell to take effect.
Have several Batteries planted a good deal of firing going on from
both sides, Boys havent yet learned the range of their French rifled
muskets. But they seem to carry up pretty well from our ridge to
the enemys works about 200 yards. None of our boys killed so far.
Several slightly wounded, Night comes again and as I have no bunk
mate I scrape the snow and wet leaves away, Wrapped in my blanket
lay down for sleep;In sleep we forget the dangers of the hour we
are exposed to.

Feb 15th.

We were aroused at 2 o'clock this morning by sharp picket firing and the command to "fall in." Threw off our snow covered blankets while the chill wintry air penetrated our very bones. We formed in line but the fire slackened;so we started fires down under the hill and gathered around them,But another spurt of firing brought us into line again. About day break we made coffee and distributed it to the men as they stood in ranks.Shortly after a close quick volley came striking down five men of Co "K. the extreme left of our Regt, This was the first time we had stood in line of battle and faced death, I looked at those men,There they lay on the snow just as they had fallen,Were they dead?, Yes, I could hardly realize it, They were so still. The wind scarcely moved the capes of their coats, They were so motionless. They moved not, Yes, these men were dead. Struck down by the first volley, What a feeling crept over me.This was war in deadly earnest, Scattering firing now began off to the right and in our front.As I was a drummer, Up to this time was merely a spectator and remained near my Company, My drum was in the snow with about four inches on the head and became the spoil of war as I never saw it afterwards,Most of the boys had on grey uniforms except our long light blue overcoats, I pulled on a pair of blue pants over the grey as private Wright called the rebels over there "Men in buckrum", About this time a German boy of Company "I was hit just below the eye,Sitting in the snow and looking very dismal.So I took his cat'ridge box buckled it around my waist and grasped his musket, I was now fully armed and equipped, The Capt pointed with his sword an and I took place in line with the file closers, These heavy 69 calibre bullets striking a man about 'midship would surely wreck the human frame! Our line was in rather a semicircle just at the crest of the ridge, flag in the center, Co "B is the color Company, Co"I next left, We are facing nearly north, Firing now to the right is getting pretty lively, along our front also, Fife Major Wright is busy getting up ammunition to the line, I dont know where the other musicians are but supposed they were helping with the wounded,Men are now being hit as a steady fire is rageing all along the lines, I got up so as to get several shots through the smoke,It was hard to see them as they kept close under their side of the ridge, Bullets were cutting through our ranks, ----

-----about this time Joe Walker with a cat.ridge in his teeth,was shot
clean through the temples, falling dead, The first man of the Co killed.
"close up" was the word, We kept the line but the boys were standing,
kneeling, and crouching most any way keeping up a roar of musketry.
Heavy firing to the extreme right seemed to be coming nearer, The 25th,
Kentucky passed in our rear going to renforce them, These Regts getting
short of amunition were forced back by the pressure of the rebel Inftry,
Swartz battery of six guns is taken, During a lull in the firing we
rested leaning on our muskets.A man came along from the right having a
squrrel tail in his cap. He stood a while looking towards the firing,
Seemed so cool and brave we were much ehcouraged, The right was now driven
back, And the enemy struck the 31st Ills, I leaned on my musket and
watched the 31st boys fight,There line seemed to be broken considerably
but taking their colors for a center they gathered around the flag and
hung to it as long as they hadamunition,encouraged by Col Logan's highly
expressive and forcible language. The brave Colonel swung his sword and
closed them up,(being himself wounded in the arm,) Finally their cat'ridge
exausted they gave way and fell back under cover of the next line of hils
Then the enemys undivided attention was turned upon us , We in the mean-
time had kept up our share of the racket, the boys falling cohtinually,
"close up" was the word, About the hardest thing I know of in battle is
to take a fallen mans place to step up and fill a gap in the ranks that
was made by the fatal bullet. While looking at Logan I was standing in
the line of file closers. Alex Hesse on one knee in the rear rank in
front of me was hit in the shoulder; the bullet went clear through and
lodged in the skin of the blade, He looked up at me put his hand to his
shoulder turned and walked out of the ranks without a word.. (I never saw
him afterwards) Shortly after this we were all engaged, I did not hear a
man groan or cry with pain that day, The wounded walked or crawled away
down the hill where the Doctors were stationed to give them attention,
The dead lay where they fell'. The constant "spang, spang" of the
muskets on the damp frosty air blending with the roar of Taylors guns,
The heavy thunder of the water batteries and Uncle Sam's Gun Boats made a
noise that was deafening, round shot would pass over our heads cutting
down timber far to the rear. The snow was trodden down and stained with the
crimson life blood of so many of our brave boys.We closed up , Keeping
the colors for our center,----

(40)

   ---And by so doing left a gap between us and the next Regt to our left.

   As the other Regiments were driven back our front was changed so
the right wing was facing nearly east, The left wing still faced
north with the colors at the angle. Our color bearer is a tall six
footer. He was shot through the fleshy part back of the hips,
Another bullet went through one foot and the final one skipped the
top of his head and downed him,but not dead, It was now noon and
they were pressing us sorely. We had orders sent to give way and fall
back, but the messenger never reached us, None of us thought of any
thing else but to hold the position at any and all hazards,The fact
is we did not know enough of war to run away, So we hung on , Some
of the boys were getting out of ammunition, I had a pretty good
supply yet, some in my pockets and several rounds in my cat'ridge
box, I changed muskets several times, Whenever I saw a brighter one
lying on the ground that some fellow had dropped when leaving the
ranks wounded. I would pick it up and fire into the smoke and brush
to the front. They knowing the ground could evidently see us better
than we could see them.I noticed the Officers were not exposing them
selves to the enemys fire any more than the boys in ranks. We were
all using the brow of the ridge to the best advantage in protecting
our bodys from the bullets, and yet the boys were getting hit in the
head so often, as the other parts of the body were not so much
exposed,By 2 P M, Forrest's Cavalry cut out and got away through the
gap in the lines, The Rebel Infantry at the same time charged ,
Sweeping up the other slope of the ridge, And being so earnest in
the matter we gave way, There was no order given that I heard,The
whole line just seemed to melt away and scatter, There was a blind
rush to get away on our part,And a forward rush on their part to get
us, (I never did understand that movement),As I saw the right wing
trying to get down in the ravine and the left breaking off that way,
I turned with my musket at a trail,As it happened the bayonet ran
in under a small jack oak tree that had been cut down and left
hanging to the stump, Some of the boys crowded in behind me and I
was forced to let loose of my musket, for I could'nt back out, So had
to go on without it. I ran down the ravine and started on up the
opposite slope, My shoes slipping in the snow for by this time the
sun was breaking out and thawing a little, -----

(41)

----Tho bullets were cutting the snow on both sides and nipping off the
twigs on the bushes and trees all around me, Color Corpl Stenger
was near me shot in both arms and one leg but kept right on, His cap
fell off, knocked off by a bullet or limb, He stopped to pick ot up,
The second time it fell off he let it go, We were now pretty well up
the slope of the opposite hill from the battle line, I looked back.
On the ground we had just occupied was a solid line of rebel Infantry
and it seemed to me every man was in the act of firing, I hurried on,
just then a musket ball struck the point of my right hip bone,stingig
like a bee, As it did not interfere with my running I kept on and was
soon over the hill and shelter from those hissing bullets,that seemed
so determind to find a target, I found the bullet had gone clean
through my over coat, coat, and under clothing, not breaking the skin
but making a beautiful round red spot about the size of a ten cent
piece, Well" I am very proud of this!"As the color bearer went down
Billy Morris grabed the colors and bore them from the field, bullet
slitted and blood stained, One bullet had cut the staff nearly intowo
The boys to the left got mixed in with Forrest's Cavalry and had some
narrow escapes, One shot at Crayton missed his face and cut holes
through the cape of his overcoat that he had rolled around his neck.
Some to the right were taken prisoner, But the most of us got out,
As I reached the top of the hill I saw long lines of Blue Inftry.
Perpendicular to our line standing at an order waiting for the enemy.
The woods seemed full of men all drifting to the rear, wounded men
assisted by comrades moving slowly and sullenly, We felt we were
whipped, the shame of it ground us. We could'ant bear it, I soon over
took Whitfield with three bullets through one leg limping along, he
threw one arm over my shoulder I grabbed his hand"Ouch", I looked and
the middle finger was hanging by a shred of skin on each side where
a musket ball had gone through, He had a glove on this hand, We came
down to a farm house, already full of wounded men ,while the Doctors
or Surgeons were quite busy, Billy Green of our Co was bare headed
holding one hand with a bleeding thumb, Going around swearing at the
rebels, the Doctors, the Government. and every thing else. Frank
Eagan was hit eleven times, Our First Lieut walked part of the way
with me picking bones out of the roof of his mouth, He was shot
through just below the temples, back of the eyes, 2d Lieut Dean was--

--------struck square in the fore head at the top of the nose, the musket
ball flattened, knocked him down. Capt Shaw is killed, Nearly every
man has bullet holes in his clothes.We passed by this farm house,
A beautiful spring of clear water, near the out buildings, this valley
of wounds and death,out of range of cannon shot and on the side hill

well up the valley We stacked arms just 116 of us left out of about

750 men that stood in line this morning.   We built up fires, ate
what little we happened to have with us some had hard bread, I had
 nothing but the cat'ridge box and belt around my waist, my long
blue overcoat and two pair pants on . We scraped away the snow and
managed to get some dry oak leaves under. We lay down on these,
three of us with one blanket to cover, We spooned up pretty close
and went to sleep,(as it was night). Many were wounded and nearly
all had bullet holes in their clothes, We slept as all tired worn
out boys naturally would until morning.   *Was 19 years old*

#####

Feb 16th, I got up early, We all fully expected that the fighting would
go on, I walked up the valley until I came to the farm house, The
sheds and every kind of shelter was filled with wounded men, I passed
on and started for the battle ground hopeing to find my knapsack
and blankets, I could hear no sound of firsing in any direction and
wondered what it could mean, As I reached the hill top just back of o
our fighting line I could see white flags along the enemys rifle
pits and concluded they had surrendered. This was quite a relief from
the pressure of supposing we had more fighting to do this day after
such a round up as we had yesterday.This being Sunday morning,
I soon reached our position, It seems the rebels had plundered our
dead, taken some prisoners and afterwards fell back to their own
intrenchments, At sun rise putting out the white flags,our wounded
men had lain all night in the snow, This in a measure stopped the
flow of blood of those most severely wounded. Capt Shaw in the act of
jumping over a log was shot through the heart and fell on his face,
The rebels had taken his sword, uniform coat, and boots, besides his
gold watch, He was a fine man and a brave Officer, We regreted his
loss to the Company so much. I found a dead man rolled up in my

---blankets, He was shot through the stomach . had wrapped himself in the

blankets laid down in a little hollow place for shelter and died during

during the night, I took one of the blankets and left him the other.

My drum that I left in the snow was gone, never saw it again. We had

a cornet band with the Regt, as well as the Drum corps, The instruments

had been pounded over the logs and hammered flat, They evidently had

no use for silver cornets, We relieved the wounded as fast as possible

,Many of the boys being now on the field. I found John Coffee the " &

extra juty man",lying there,"Well John what can I do for you, and are

you badly hurt","Oh! Me arrum and me side,could you get me a wee drop

of whiskey", His voice was thick and his lips blue with the cold

and suffering, "Yes indeed?. I procured a tin cup full of good strong

commisary whiskey he drank it down, There never was a drink of whiskey

that did a man so much real good as that did, and he never forgot it

either. I could not find my knapsack so I had only one blanket left.

We helped get the wounded away as soon as possible that they might

have some care. Just a little ways below our line we found a rebel

that had been wounded placed by his comrades near a fire, During the

night he had rolled into the fire and his abdomen was all burned out.

died A blackened corpse. others were partly frozen, One of Co E" men shot
through the lung, died
froze while lying there with his back to the field. A stream of blood and foam ran out of his mouth and

The forces in the Fort and intrenchments surrendered to day, About

13000 laid down their arms, In the Fort there is 13 heavy guns, two

that carry 128# balls, besides 81 pieces of light artillery in and

around the breast works, I went through the mud on over to Dover a

small town, The place is full of rebel soldiers, They are taking

them on the Steamers for Cairo, said they "were going North to spend

the summer", One rebel Captain said as we went farther south we would

catch the " very mischief",I saw piles of muskets, squirrel rifles. an

and a lot of fine shot guns. some silver mounted. a good many of these
(Our Government has no use for such an assorted supply of arms)
were sent home by the boys A soldier would come along pick up a rifle

or musket look at it throw it down on the pile, "whang!" it would go

off sending a bullet singing off in most any direction, It seems

they are all loaded, left so by the secesh.No guard to look after

them, piled up like cord wood.Managed to get up a few tents and here

we are in a wedge tent all so cross and grouty cant keep from quarrel

ing about every thing, The rattle of a leaf startles us , any rasping

sound sets the shivers going, Sounds like the whistle of a -----

---bullet, I reckon we're nervous.

Feb 17th, Went over to the Battle ground, The trees and bushes are cut
and splintered, Good sized saplings are cut down by musket balls

alone, Once during the fight I heard a shower of canister shot
pass over our Heads, Some shell and solid shot, But we payed no
attention to these, The bullet is what counts, Gathered our dead,
A trench six feet wide was dug and the dead laid in side by side,
They were then covered with blankets, A few words by the Chaplin,
The trench is then filled with earth, 78 were buried in this one
grave on the line where they fell. all from our Regt, Some of the
wounded have died and probably more will die. I lost my journal
from jany 1st or part of it. also my port folio with stamps, paper.
gold pen.silver holder, Some of the Rebels got it with my knapsack,
(Joe Walker shot through the temples with a cat'ridge in his teeth.
fell over on one of the boys, the blood spouting over his coat,
They dragged him a little to one side or down the hill, Joe's
Brother, A member of the 45th Ills of our Brigade, came to see
him we showed him where Joe lay,,I saw him stand and look at his
Brother lying there dead, He said nothing and soon turned away
and left him there .Going back to his own Regt,)
Details of rebels performed the last sad rights for their dead
also, And so they buried the slain,At our grave boards were set
up at the head of each with name and Company cut there on,

Feb 18th, Pleasant, the mud is drying up fast, Some of the prisoners are
yet buring their dead,

Feb 19th, Cloudy and raining nearly all day, A good many of the boys
are sick, The wounded are getting along fairly well , many
have gone to the Mound City Hospital, Both of our Lieuts have
gone home. Lieut Dean with the Captains. body. Our Company and
the Regt for that matter are in a miserable condition , sick,
wounded and so many killed , some taken prisoner makes it a
gloomy time for us,

Moral; We attacked an intrenched position, And won or gained it

No 44 B
   Our loss at the Battle of Ft Donelson, Tenn,
   Feb 15th 1862,

1 Capt Fred W Shaw,   (Killed),
2 Private Joe Walker,   "   "

3 1st Lieut A R Wilcox,   Wounded. (Died of wounds),
4 Private John Vaughn,   "   " "   "   "

5 2d Lieut Sam B Dean,   "   " (Bullet flattened on forehead)
6 1st Sergt Jas D Vernay,   "   " (Taken Prisoner),(bullet through
7 Private J S Lincott,   "   "   "   "   " right arm)
8   "   "   Dan McMahon,   "   "   "   "   "

9 2d Sergt J W Larr,   "   "
10 4th "   C A Blackburn,   "   "
11 1st Corpl E T Coleman,   "   "
12 5th Col " D Stenger,   "   " (Both arms) and leg)

13 Musician G D Carrington,   "   " (Slightly)

   Privates
14 Barnhart Jacob,   "   "
15 Coffee John,   "   " (Arm & side)
16 Crane C W,   "   "
17 Eagan Francis,   "   " (Eleven wounds)
18 Green Wm J,   "   " (Thumb)
19 Hesse Alexander,   "   " (Through shoulder)
20 Hester Frank,   "   "
21 Linscott Anthony.   "   "
22 Larkins Tho B,   "   "
23 Murray J B,   "   " (Slightly)
24 Madden Jas H,   "   " "   "
25 Plummer William.   "   "
26 Powers John H,   "   "
27 Peck Warren,   "   " (Slightly, Buck Shot)
28 Springer David,   "   " "   "
29 Whitfield Alfred,   "   " (Leg & hand)

The expression,Our Regt is "cut to pieces" Means a loss in battle
of 30 to 50 %, And yet a Regt may in battle loose killed,wounded,
missing,taken prisoner,and scattered, And after the battle get together
and only have a loss of 10%, While they really thought they were
 "Cut to pieces", The morning report generally tells the story,
The holding on of a Regt in a given position with a great sacrifice
in its numbers may be of great benefit to the other Regts engaged,
Like the individual who looses his own life to save others,

Feb 2oth,.Rather cool, ground frozen a little, wrote a letter to Father,

Feb 21st,   Went all around this side of the fortifications. Saw piles
            of old flint lock muskets and other secesh things,

Feb 22d, Raining with some thunder, We are cooped up in our tent,
            its so bad to get around,

Feb 23d, Pleasant and clear; Hope it will quit raining for a day or so
            at least, Going down to the steamer Uncle Sam to unload our mess
            chests, have a tin plate now to eat grub half way decent, and
            maybe a fork,with our Fremont tents,

Feb 28th, Nothing much going on we are quietly in camp, getting straight-
            end out ,There is to be a muster for pay, rec'd a letter from home.

        March 1st, 1862. Fort Donelson Tenn. Cool and cloudy, The Sutler
            ppened up his goods , Took a dollars worth of tickets, The first
            for the begining of the three years service, Under marching
            orders,

March 2d Sunday, Raining out side, Drv and comfortable in our large

            Fremont tent, old Bill cooking breakfast of coffee, pancakes, and
            a good supply of grease, Not leave camp to day I suppose, Our 1st
            Sergt Vernay came back from Nashville, with two privates, They were
            wounded and taken prisoner, They were left at the above place while
            those not wounded were taken on South, The Sergt'sright arm was
            badly hurt a bullet passed through the fleshy part between the
            shoulder and elbow, He being a free Mason, found friends and was
            cared for, We were glad to have him with us again, As we have ho
            Commissioned Officers with the Company,

March 3d,
Talk of leaving, packed up our mess chests and got them aboard the Boat,
march in the morning no telling where,

March 4th,
            Left camp at the Fort about 8 this morning, rain and cold,
took the road towards Fort Henry and marched until we reached an old
smelting furnace where we made our bivouac for the night,

March 5th, Leave for the Tennessee River, Regt gone, sitting by the fire
waiting for the wagons, some time in the night I had a queer presentiment,
of something going to happen, could not tell whether it concerned me
personally, or others, I mentioned it to a comrade, sun shines and pleasant,
Wagons came at last, we reached the river and went aboard the Steamer
Memphis,

March 6th,
On board the Boat and not off yet,

March 7th, On the boat a few miles above Fort Henry,
            lay here all night,

March 8th&9th, Loyed around on the Boat about half sick, not off yet,
            noticed a lot of rags in gunny sacks along the cabin deck,
nice to sleep on, some of the folks up North have sent these rags for the
wounded, wish they had sent us some thing we could eat when sick,
March 1oth,   (on orderly),
Still on the old Memphis, no movement yet, cold and raining, good many
sick, will be payed off in a few days,

March 11th,
            The old Boat is making good time now, getting along first
rate, the people along the river seem delighted to see us, swinging their
hats and hankerchiefs, or maybe they never saw so many Boats and soldiers,
Cane along the river in large groves or breaks, also high bluffs, rock,
and pine trees,

March 12th,
            Stopped for the night , tied up on the west bank of the river,
some of the Regt have landed, pleasant and beautiful country, some 3oo
on the other side of the river have enlisted for the Union, there is 65
Boats in all on this expedition all loaded with soldiers, rations and
amunition, received a letter from home,

March 13th,
            Landed and the Regt camped for the night about one mile from the
    river, near the town of Savannah,
March 14th, I remained on the Boat last night, sick, left the Boat and
reached our tents, camped on a muddy side hill field, crawled in and
layed down, commenced raining rained all night, some of the boys went out
and slept in some old barns, left us in the tent so we could find a dry
March 15th, Nothing but mud and rain,   / place to sleep,

 March 18th, Savannah Tenn, Camped a little east of town, quite pleasant
and sun shines, warm spring like. The secesh are plundering and hanging
every Union man in the country, they go in roving bands and make it their
business to plunder and rob Union people, this kind of work should be
stopped,

March 21st, Cool weather, Taylors Battery leave to day, suppose we will
go soon, a good many sick in camp, (Jacob W Groves died)
our Co on picket, recruiting going on , Capt Waddell of Co E has some 2o or
25 recruits, Tennessee men and some from Alabama, they make good soldiers,
rainy wet and cool, Oh I wish I wasent in "Dixie" better times coming boys,

March 23d, Leave Savannah to day, marched down and are now on board

-- the Steamer Uncle Sam, Started up the river,

March 24th, Landed at Pittsburg Landing this morning, Got off the Boat and
marched out about 3 or 4 miles where we have piched out tents h
in the woods, A pleasant place to camp with plenty of wood and
water, Our line is about five miles long , Well'it is getting
late and a long time after tattoo, I must retire for we may
have to march tomorrow,

March 25th, Camp of the Woods, About 18 miles from Corinth, The rebels are
said to be fortifying and have a large force commanded by Genl
Johnson and Beaureguard, They may make a stand, But the future
will tell,Bed time (Genl Sherman reviewed his Brigade to day,)

March 26th, Sergt Veenay is home on furlough, Pleasant and warm, A letter
from home, We are cleaning up around camp, As I lost my drum at
Donelson I have no duty except Orderly about once a week,

March 27th,
The weather is warm and spring like, At dress parade this
evening we had out 212 men,The Regt is pretty well played out,
A good many on sick list, Mumps going the rounds. several have
                                                          them

March 28th, Quiet about Camp. Not very well.Reported that Genl Buel with
7o ooo Inftry, 3o Batteries of Artillery and 6ooo Cavalry is
only 13 miles from here,

March 31st, Sunday weather warm, past few days about the same, Sick, Not
able for duty. Have hardly any duty since the battle of Donelson

April 1st, Warm and dry, Sick lying in the tent most of the time. Quiet in
Camp,

April 2d, Rain last night, Cool this morning, Some better to day,
Boys out drilling, Nothing of interest about camp,

April 3d, Had a review of Genl McClernards' Division of three Brigades,
passed off very well, Warm clear and fine,
Ours is the 2d Brigade, Col Marsh, 11th Ills, 2oth, 48th, and
45th Ills (this last is called the Lead Mine Regt,) Taylors
six gun Battery, All Illinois Boys,

April 4th. Rain early this morning. Cleared off hot. Trees green and fruit
trees in bloom. Great talk among the Boys that the 11th is
going to be disbanded. It must be talk. Most likely is. Feel
pretty well to day. No movement as yet. Waiting for Genl Buel.
He has the promise of attacking this time. Just at dark the
Secesh have attacked our line out at the extreme front. Some
heavy firing of cannon and musketry. The Drummers beat the long
roll, each taking it up from the different camps clear on down to
the river. In less than fifteen minutes our Regt was in line and
remained in line of battle most of the night. Later the firing ceased.
All finally got quiet and we lay down for sleep. Nothing more until it
turns up.

April 5th. Clear and warm. all quiet about camp. the firing last night
resulted . (so we hear) in six being killed on the rebel side,
and four killed and twenty wounded on our side. We also took two
pieces of artillery. They supposed we had left the place and
came to see. But they found us ready and prepared for them.
Night. All quiet now, clear and cool.

April 6th, Sunday. We got up this morning as usual, Had breakfast and
were just hanging our haversacks up on the cross arms of the tent,
when we heard the sound of firing in our advance out on the Corinth
road , at first a few scattering shots then a volley of musketry,
followed by artillery, Then the drummers again beat the long roll,
That awful dismal sound, beginning out towards the front and taken
up by different Regt's from one camp to another way on down the
line clear back to the river landing,The quick forming of Regt's
 Of Infantry. Horses hitched th the guns, These great horses
galloping with the cannon to the front, Mules and wagons hurrying
th the rear. Those blood curdling sounds of the alarm drums ,
increased the excitement, volleys of musketry, the roar of the
rebel artillery, our own guns chiming in. " Ah then and there was
hurrying to and fro", Shell and solid shot plowed up the ground
tore through our tents , splintered trees falling far to the rear,
as several cannon shot passed over our camp, One cutting the hind
hoof off a horse,The Regt fell in and marched out towards the firing.
formed on the right of the Brigade with Taylors Battery to the
right where they opened fire, Through the woods came the splendid
lines of the secesh Infantry, Some of their Regt's wore blue uniform:
 and carried a blue flag with a single star in the center, Some of
our boys held their fire thinking they were our own men,Some began
firing at long range but they kept on coming, Every one was loading :
and firing as fast as possible, bullets hissing over our heads and
cutting the limbs , twigs and that peculiar chug when a bullet
strikes a man, We did'ent maintain this position very long, loosing
several men we fell back until our Company took shelter behind a
pile of oats in gunny sacks, Here we began firing on the artillery
horses, killing several,The rebels were checked by our fire, but
they seemed to drift towards our left flank, as if shunning and
dreading the tremendous fire they had to face, This movement on
their part kept our men falling back taking new positions farther
back and nearer the river landing, Being soon driven from the oats
pile the Boys got scattered, Our Company was just gone as an
organized unit, By this time it was fearful. Wounded men with
Comrades to help them were limping to the rear, Which means toward
the river,----

(49)

7-Artillery horses cut loose from the guns, Cavalry horses with saddle
under instead of over, or on their backs,Men with arms, and men with out
arms,Wagons with six mules hitched the drivers cussing and whipping, All
rushing for the rear,One of the boys asked a man of Swartz Battery "if
they spiked the guns when they left them, " Spike dose goons und spile
dose goons, Oh,no,no,"This raised a laugh,
Still the muskets volleyed and the cannon thundered, while the smoke
rolling up among the trees hid the lines at times then to drift away,
Birges rifle men (sharpshooters) filed past, they had common hunting
rifles with bullet pouches, over their shoulders, squirrel tails in
their caps, no bayonets, We felt sorry for them, could they stand
a charge , They were fine marksmen and fought mostly on their own hook,
taking trees and advantage of the ground, As we drifted to the rear
I overtook Capt Coats he had just reached camp joined in the line as he
was unarmed, A bullet struck the breast of his coat tearing out the
cotton while another hit his wrist, There was a boy with him.
(his son),I passed a man lying in a field, a piece of shell had torn
a large chunk out between the hip and knee, No one payed any attention
to the poor fellow,Our Drum Major gathered up his $30,oo drum that the
Boys had given him and put out for the river, I saw none of the other
members of the Drum Corps, No one ran, just walked on sullen, panic
stricken, The terrors hidden under that cloud of smoke,Two of our boys
sick with the mumps had stayed in camp as long as possible, They
joined me bringing their mumps with them, Pressing on towards the
river, It must be about noon we met Lewis and Drake both armed and
equiped, Drake had a bullet hole through his haversack, slightly
wounding his thigh, In the changes of position got lost from the Co.
their muskets were blackened showing they had been firing, We had a
perfect dread of fighting in other Regt.s, for if killed our friends
would never know what had become of us, As we neared the river we saw
Officers trying to get men into ranks, but they payed no attention to
them , but drifted on, There was a good many under the river bank
supposeing they were safe, Off to the south I saw a whole Regt
come rushing down the hill with the Col at the head,--thinking the
whole line was broken we turned north and kept on down the river,
One of Swartz' Battery men came along saying "Battery Swartz ish
all gone but one man and two horses",

(50)

Late in the evening our Regt, what was left, with the colors were sitting
on a log near Genl Grants Head Quarters, Our Col Wallace is reported killed.
Ransom wounded, Dead and wounded every where, And still they are coming
in, The Boys on the battle line are holding them back while the artillery
is forming in position on the hill to keep them from the landing,
As night came on rain began to fall, We managed to crawl onto a tent,
(The five of us remained together,) The rebels were in our tents a mile
or more away, Soon after dark the two Gun Boats opened fire, sending
9 inch shell up the ravine cutting off great limbs from the trees,
and utterly demoralizing the enemy. Every fifteen minutes these guns
roared all night, The pouring rain, the flash like lightning of the
cannon the scream of the shell in its flight through the woods, the
bursting report far over the rebel lines and bivouac made night hideous
in all our surroundings,(We got some sleep),

April 7th,

Morning comes at last, wet and muddy, During the night
some of Genl Buel's Regts crossed over the river, Genl Wallace
came up with his Division on our right. They all moved out to the
front, opened fire and began driving the rebels back gaining
ground until about three or four o'clock we were back in our
camp, We took no part in the second days fight, unless some of the
Boys went out sharp shooting on their own hook.We found some of the
wounded rebels had occupied our tents, making it very comfortable
for them, I counted 31 shell and bullet holes in our tent, A barrel of
hard tack standing by the center pole had pieces of shell and bullets
mixed with the hard bread, We were very glad to be back in our
Fremont tent once more. A large oak tree grew near my tent. At the
root lay an Iowa boy dead, We had a sheet iron cook stove out side
the tent bored full of holes by bullets, had to stop the holes with
mud in order to use it for cooking purposes, I counted 90 dead horses
lying in front of our Brigade line, Not far from my tent I found a
Secesh boy wounded lying on a mattress another one over him, He followed
us with his eyes thinking perhaps we would kill him, I got a canteen of
water for him, we left him there, Afterwards he was taken away and
cared for, He was shot through the stomach, and most likely died,

Dead men are scattered allthrough the woods for miles. I noticed
where batteries had been set the boys had taken off one wheel of the
guns and rolled them away, So when the rebel retreat began they had
no time to hunt up wheels, The cannon are all through the woods just
as we left them, Dresser lost two guns these were taken away by the
rebels, Taylor lost none either here or at Donelson, The 45th Ills
are armed with short Enfield rifles with sabre bayonet, I found one
of these lying in an open field with belt, cat'ridge box all complete
no one dead or living near, I was now armed and equiped, Sergt Larr
in command of the Company was killed. as the line broke Hester the
tallest man in the Company was seen crouched behind a stump
capping his musket for one more shot before he fell back,
Sergt Larr was struck in the chin and another bullet killed him,

We are orphans; Col Ransom wounded and taken to a Boat all night
long calling for his horse and sword, "Old Bob, His horse, was
killed. Major Nevius wounded, Capt Carter of Co "K killed, Lieut
Fields of Co "A wounded,The Regt went in with 200 men lost 96,
Co "H reduced to one man and a Lieut,Sergt Merriman of Co "H also
wounded,

April 8th,   Men detailed for the purpose of digging the grave buried 14
of our Regt in one grave, I did not see Sergt Larr until after
he was laid in the grave, He was lying flat on his back with one
arm, the right, thrown up with the fore arm resting on his forehead,
(across),He was always neat and soldierly in appearance, a fine
man, A good soldier, was always humming or singing while about
camp,-" In the sweet fields of Eden there is rest for the weary",
He found his rest here, Tommy Newport made a monument of oak
five or six feet high, this was set up and the names cut thereon,
Co and Regt, Letters painted black, the monument painted white,
We built a fence with poles around the grave,

April 9th, Damp and cool, All be sick if we do not get out of this,
   Burying the dead, Loud cheers along our lines as the rebel
   prisoners are coming in,Hauling in rebel dead with six mule teams.
Big Government wagons piled up with the dead, in all positions as
   they were firing or loading, so they remained stiff and cold in
   death,400 are buried near our camp,in one long trench, They are not
   all in yet, As many are scattered for miles around, lying just where
   they fell, The dead horses begin to be offensive as many of them are lying
   in the woods, We found whiskey and gun powder in the canteens of
   the enemy,Beauregard told them they must fight,for this battle
   would decide whether there was a Southern Confederacy or not, I
   think there is not, Some of them were old U S Regulars, The blue
   uniforms of the Louisana Tigers did not save them; they were driven
   back with the rest, Genl W H L Wallace was struck in the head by a
   musket ball, left on the field all night, Afterwards taken on Boat
   down to Savannah, In one of our tents the boys cared for a little
   Irishman who was wounded in the foot; He was quite cheerful, Smoking
   his pipe and lying on the blankets; He belonged to a Secesh Regt.
It was reported among the soldiers that Genl Beauregard said at
   the begining of the battle "I would water my horse in the Tennessee
   river that night or in h----." Well;I guess he did not reach the
   drinking place that day,
They used canister shot, This is fixed amunition, A red flanel bag
of powder fastened to a block of wood which is also the bottom of the
tin can that fits the bore of the gun, This can is filled with iron
balls about an inch in diameter. At the discharge the can is torn and
the balls scatter like shot from a shot gun,
The expression;"give them grape,"is really not as correct as to say,"give
them canister," as this was used more than grape,
Shrapnel is shells filled with iron balls about as large as musket
balls. When the shell explodes these fly in all directions, but with
more force straight ahead,
All these are used mostly by field guns, 6 pounders. 12 pounders.
and 24 pounders. The short Howitzer is a shell gun exclusively,
The Rebel artillery used round shot and also elongated solid shot and
shell.

(53)

April 10th,   men
        We are yet in camp, same place; dead horses and are yet in the
woods and fields, muskets that have been bent by striking trees, piles of
cartridge boxes, that have been cut off the dead, cannon caissions,
equipments of all kinds, when the rebels came across a bright musket,
they would throw down their old Harpers Ferry muskets, and take ours,
of the same calibre, (69), thus supplying themselves with better ones,
Theyhad a fashion ofplacing a long plug of natural leaf tobacco in the
inside breast pocket of their Jackets, during the fighting they could
reach down and bite off a chew, we found so many of these plugs in the
pockets of the dead, A brass button with the word Mississipi in a circle
around the edge, a single star in the centre, came into my posession,
cut off the coat of a dead rebel soldier,

April 11th,
        Genl Wallace died last night, of his wounds, he was a brave man
and well beloved by the Regt and Brigade; we are so few we are getting
fearful of being consolidated with some other Regt and so loose our
number; Sergt Geo Shaw is in command of the Co,
    John w Larr, killed,
    Henry Connells, Missing in action,
    Francis M Hester, wounded.
    Andrew Drake, slightly wounded,

    (17 men left in the Company, about 150 men in the Regt,)

    Trees and bushes are scared and splintered with bullets, and cannon shot,
    I saw several rammers sticking in trees, In the excitement of loading
and firing many forgot to return rammer after loading, a ramrod will
whistle as well as a bullet, and kill just the same,

April 12th, Raining ,wet and disagreeable, the battered Regts are getting
straightend out, hardly men enough for duty in our Co, only one or two
drums in the Regt, the Drum Major beats the calls, no one seems to
bother with me, am on "orderly" occasionally is all the duty I have to do,

April 13th,
            Warm and pleasant. ground is wet but a few days of sun shine
            will make it dry, P M the Regt on parade, pretty slim line,
            to what it once was, No news,

    April 14th, Pleasant, warm, all quiet on Owl Creek,

    April 15th. John Coffee returned to the Co, (his arm hanging, not much
use,) to get his discharged from the service; he was glad to see me,

J J, Stuart returned to get his discharge for disability; poor John not
very stout yet; he was so sick when he left us at Camp Birds Point, I
    hardly expected to see him again,
    Dave Stenger also returned; his arms are much swollen yet, from the Fort
Donelson bullets; he is color Corpl; we have now earned our battle flag,
the Blue Banner, the old flag was sent home with Col Wallace' body,

April 16th, John Coffee ,(Irishman) "sez he to me, what? and so we went
way out and sat down on a log, in the woods, he moved aside the cape of
his blue overcoat and there was a rubber canteen full of whiskey, where
 in the world he ever got that none but an Irishman could tell, as whiskey
 was a forbiden article, except for Hospital and Officers use, in camp,
    In those days I did not drink ,Iwas sorry for his sake, he wanted to do
    something for me ,remembering the tin cup full at Donelson,

April 18th,
  We have good news from all over the country of victorys gained by our
troops, McClellan is before York_town; is not taken yet, Boys in pretty
good spirits but not over anxious for another battle, Our Regt is to badly
played out to ever stand another hard fight, but what is left are good
and will stand fire, Change guns to-day,
Turned over the heavy French rifled musket, and drew English Enfield
rifles, round bands, and longer stocks than our old ones, calibre 58,
  My short Enfield is the same, Our drill changed from Scotts to Hardee,
but as the secesh drill Hardee we changed Casey, we now march in fours,
instead of twos, the Co is more compact, and not so strung out as by twos,
these fours are called Comrades in battle, the piece is carried in the
right hand, instead of the left, grasped at the small of the stock,
resting in the hollow of the right shoulder,

(Genl Grant and myself are very much alike, He is a Genl without a command,
And I am a drummer without a drum.)

  April 2oth,
          Rained all last night, wet and muddy this morning,
          Camp on owl creek quiet,

  April 22d, Just one year ago to day that I enlisted in Uncle Sams service;
          it was a pleasent and beautiful morning in Lacon Ills.;
          it is cool damp and muddy here,

  April 24th, *Begining of Siege of Corinth.*
          Moved out about two miles, our Brigade, and others,
here we began digging, constructing breast works, useing logs and poles,
as a frame work , using the earth to cover and fill, leaving a ditch to
stand in, we are preparing for the Secesh as fast as possible,

April 25th, Rain,, rain and mud,

April 26th,
          The sun rose this morning beautiful and clear, No news,

Immense cheering along our lines, New Orleans said to be taken by the
Yankees, P M, All quiet on Owl Creek,

April 29th, Moved out about two or three miles and camped in line of battle,

April 30th, Raining this morning, are to be mustered for pay , we will
probably wait here a day or so, to bring up the rear, are advancing very
caustiously on Corinth, Beauregaurd is known to have a large force there,
Two Regts of Secesh laid down their armes and gave themselves up as
prisoners of war; tired of the service in the Rebel ranks,

May 1st, Seven years ago to day since I came to Ills,

May 2d, Pleasant and warm, getting ready for the coming battle, fast as po
possible, No news,
May 3d, Sound of Cannon and musketry out near Farmington,
May 4th, Sunday,   must be some fighting going on,
                  Packed up for a start towards Corinth,
Marched about two miles, commenced raining, rained, roads all mud,
finally got to our camp ground, built up fires and tryed to dry out some
of the wet, our tents came up at last, got them set and went to bed,
rained nearly all night, had several small streams running through our tent,

May 5th, Got up this morning wet, with mud in the tent about three inches
deep, later its drying,

May 6th, One month to day since the great battle of Pittsburg Landing,
pleasant this afternoon, drying fast, got out several of our seige guns,
on the road to Corinth, they have big high weels with the gun slung
under the axl tree, and all the horses and mules hitched to them that can

possibly pull a pound, and then they stick in the mud,

May 7th, Review of our Brigade, 2d of the Third First Division,weather fine and roads drying fast,Boys in good spirit,
Afternoon Genl McClernard, made a speech to the division and among other things he said Yorktown has surrendered and the rebels had fallen back to Richmond, They have a way of getting whiskey into camp for the knowing ones, you buy a squaretin can of oysters, (and there you are)
May 8th, Mississipi,camp,
Cannonading and musketry out towards Farmington, off to our left.

May 11th,Sunday, Leave camp to day,on the road to Corinth,will this Sunday moving ever be done with, The battle will not come off for a day or two at least, Sunday evening arrived at our camping place, and quietly settle down again, no attack as yet,

May 14th, Some cannonading out towards Corinth, said to be fighting over a stream of water, our men wanted water,and the rebels wanted water too, had a fight and secesh skedaddled,No movement of importunce so far as I know, all quiet now,

May 15th, Very warm and dry weather now,,water getting scarse,
Manny of the boys sick in camp, Paymaster came around, after signing the rolls, we march up to the table as our names are called, and payed off, four months pay, I received $48,oo, not much chance to spend money here ,boys manage to have a little game of poker or seven up among themselves, more to pass time than for the money,
May 16th,
(Camp near Monteray)

May 18th Sunday,Cool and pleasant, three Companies gone out on picket or put post duty, some heavy firing on our right yesterday afternoon between pickets, received a letter from home, can hear the boom of heavy guns every once in a while,
wrote home sent $5,oo in letter,
(We are now the 3d Brigade, of the 1st Division,) Reserve.composed of the (cut up) Regts, mostly from Illd.
May 19th, Regts have all gone,ours is left to guard camp, heavy firing away off to the right and left, suppose the ball has opened, cool day looks some like rain, good day to fight will not suffer for water, as it is very scarce,now and then a gun out towards Corinth,

May 20th, Rain last night, cool to day,some heavy firing this morning, all quiet now, Boys just came in from picket,One of Co "D'S men wounded, last night,(shot through the arm,)
May 21st, Some heavy firing this mornong, Move to day ,
P M quiet and pleasant,

May 24th, Quietly in camp last few days,we are left in the rear to guard commissary stores, damp and cool,
Ransom is promoted Colonel and is on McClernards staff rank of Inspector Genl,

Trees are green, peaches and apples are large as walnuts.wheat is headed out and will soon be ready to cut, There is another harvest nearly ready, Uncle Sams Soldiers will be the reapers,

May 25th, Sunday, Working on the breast works as usual, The Army advances
          a short distance then go to building rifle pits and breast works,
          We act awful scarey, Weather pleasant. Our Company came in from
          picket.

May 26th, A letter from home.

May 27th Slowly moving forward, We are in the reserve and do guard duty,
     and picket, build breast works &c,The health of the camp is pretty good.
          From what we can learn the rebels in Corinth are hard up for grub,"
          also a scarcety of water, Our men and the secesh" had a fight over a
          creek a few days ago, They were driven off and our men use the water,
          It is poor and hard to find enough to supply the Army,
          Weather hot with cool nights, No planting here the fields are
          ·trampled down, Cut up by the heavy army wagons, Artillery &c,
          Pails are being burned for camp fires, There is plenty of hogs
          running through the woods but we are not allowed to kill them,
          Firing between the out posts and pickets, When Genl Halleck gets
          his plans laid all right there will be some fighting here,
          We can buy bread from the bread wagon at 10 cents a loaf about as
          big as two biscuits, butter is 40 cents pr pound,

May 28th, Our Co on picket, will be in to day, hot and dry, some prospect
               of a battle, Heavy firing off to the left,

May 29th, Moved camp out about two miles,, Heavy firing all day,
               Drove the secesh about a mile, hot,and water scarce, muddy what
               we do get.

May 30th,   Some firing this morning, Reported that Corinth is evacuated,
               13000 prisoners, Orders to march at a moments notice with
               four days rations, and 100 rounds of cat'ridges to each man,

May 31st
               Corinth is ours, The secesh left yesterday, Pope is hard
               after them, No prisoners, They burned every thing of value.
               and have fallen back on Jackson Miss, Warm and dry, no
               water.

June 1st,   Sunday, Cool and dry, some appearance of rain, Divine service
               at Col Nevius' Head Quarters at 10 A M, To day passed off
               very well, Talk of our Regt going to Ills to recruit in health
               as well in numbers,

June 2d,   Our Regt on picket duty, pleasant and cool, Boys enjoying _____

Playing cards on the ralling post, The merry month of May has gone ,

June hot and dusty has come in this climate with slim chance for water,

   We poor soldier boys will have to suffer some. We have stood the cold,

      think we can stand the heat, all quiet here, secesh all far away,

June 3d,   Rained nearly all last night, boys all wet. I got some boards

         . and made a kind of a shelter that kept two of us fairly dry

         all night, Sun shines this morning.Pleasant once more,

         Releived about 8 A M, by the 2oth Regt. Ills Inftry,

June 4th,   Left camp about 1o o'clock this morning, Marched some thing

            like 1o miles, Our teams did not come up with the camp out

            fit, So we had to sleep without tents, Slept very well however

            considering the ants and wood ticks that crawled over us

            during the night,

June 5th, Started out this morning, Did not march very far,Found us in a

            new Brigade of the 11th, 2oth, 29th, and 45th, all Illinois Regi

            and good ones at that, Passed through a pretty fine country,

            corn crop looks well,Marched through a small town called Purdy,

            Quite a nice little town, Camped for the night about a mile

            from the Rail Road,Fences covered with " blacks and white

            children looking at the soldiers marching by,the bands playing,

June 6th, Arrived at Bethel a town on the Railroad, about noon, and camped

            about half mile farther on in an old secesh camp. Got dinner

            set up our tent, Have to go on picket in an hour, felt the shock

            of an earth quake about 1o 3o this morning while resting along

            the road, I was sitting with my back to a hickory sapling,

            When I noticed the swaying of the earth, making a pecular

            sickening sensation pass over me,

            Saw the graves of two men that belonged to the 41st Georgia,

            Regt, Died of sickness, Cars just came in , Road is all clear

            from Corinth to Jackson Tenn, Looks some like rain,

            Black women and old men are at work in the corn fields, Young

            men all in the secesh" army, Some of them charged 6o cents for

            a canteen full of milk, and 25 cents for a small loaf of corn

            bread,Here they charge us 5 cents for a cup full of milk.

            1o cents for loaf of corn bread, a " pone" as they call it,
            good water and plenty,

June 7th,

Got up this morning about 4 o'clock and by day light were on the march, Suppose we were going to Boliver, but took the Jackson road,Marched about 20 miles, Saw some pretty fine country, Cutting wheat and plowing corn seems to occupy the time of the people left at home.

June 8th, On the march, 15 miles from Jackson, Will get there to day no bad luck, Seems to be a strong Union sentiment through this part of Tenn,Arrived at Jackson about sun down, Quite a large place, Captured some commissary stores, but did not succeed in getting any rebels,

June 9th, Camped in Jackson, Our tents came through on the cars, We have them up. In quite a pleasant place, Good water and plenty of wood,

June 10th, Rec'd letters and papers from home, Warm but pleasant, We draw flour now instead of hard bread. So we got hold of some brick and built ovens, using mud for mortar, I make biscuit,and blackberry pie, as blackberries are quite plentiful growing along the Rail road mostly, I get sour milk of the citizens to mix the flour, put in some soda, roll out the dough, make very good biscuits, build a fire in the oven then when it is hot rake out the coals and put in the bread and pies, Bake just as nice as they do at home,

June 11th, Had an alarm last night, One man shot by the pickets, through a mistake or some thing else, Letter from home.

June 12th, All quiet about camp, Boys drilling this morning, Co"B and Co "H are together as one Company, Sergt Merriman of Co "H is absent sick in Hospital.

This is the hottest Secesh" place we have been in yet, The C Citizens wont hardly look at us especially the Women, The Darkeys take the town, As we marched in on Sunday the streets were alive with them, Dressed to kill, In the best and finest, Most of the white men are Officers in the rebel Army, Some of the prices in this town are rather high, butter 50 cents, milk 25 cents per quart, biscuit 5 cents each, flour $12, per barrel $20, for a pair of boots, soda 90 cents per pound, tobacco $1. plug, and every thing in proportion, Salt and coffee can not be

--had only as the Union Army soldiers brong it in, 60 Hogsheads of sugar
were captured and other Army stores,

June 13th, As I have no drum since the battle of Donelson, My duties are
very light, on orderly about once a week, There is only two or
three drums in the drum corps, No one pays very much attention
to me , I do about as I please, Cook for a mess, clean up around,
and hang to the short Enfield, I picked up at Shiloh, I enlisted
as a musician, Am not called upon for other duty,

June 14th, Not very well, Hot and very dusty, Our Co on picket,

June 15th, Sunday morning cool and pleasant, All quiet about camp.and town,
Boys will soon be in from picket, Feel pretty well to day,

June 16th, Several Regt's came in this evening, Two Batteries of artillery,
Cavalry and wagons, The Boys looked dusty and tired having
marched 20 miles , Good marching through the dust and hot sun,

June 17th Corn is in tassle, New potatoes, and blackberries plenty,
A few ripe apples, They are planting out large fields of corn
By order from Jeff Davis",

June 18th, Rained last night, cool and pleasant this morning, Companies
"I,F,and "K have gone up to Humboldt, A town on the Mobile &
Ohio, R,R, about 18 miles above here, The cars come in regularly
from Corinth, at about 1 o'clock A M each day bringing the
mail, Soldiers, forage &c,

June 19th,   Pleasant, The usual camp life,

June 22d,   Past few days hot and not much change in our duties,
Sunday, all quiet, hot and dusty, Went down to the Forkadeer
creek had a swim, Then picked some blackberries,returned to
camp,

June 24th, Cool and cloudy, There is to be a review of our Brigade,
The line formed at 6 A M, Passed in review before Genl Ransom,
Our old Colonel,

June 25th, I concluded it would be better for me to go into the ranks,
So I marched up to Col Nevius' tent and asked him permission
to go into the ranks as private, He says "George there is so few
drummers like to have you stay in the drum corps", But as I
insisted he gave consent So I reported to Sergt Shaw, High ___ .

(60)

-Private for duty, Took my place in rear rank left of the of the Co'!

June 26th,
Detailed for picket first thing this morning,after the
guard was formed marched down to the bridge south of town,
Stacked arms, posted the guard then went in and had a good swim,
after marching through the dust and heat, My turn came,was on
two hours from 1o to 12 midnight), Passed off quietly.

June 27th, Releived at 1o o'clock and returned to camp. Quiet about camp
and town, None of us are allowed to leave as we may have orders
to march any time,

June 28th, Hot and dry, Letters from home, The Mobile & Ohio R R .Is open
from Corinth to Columbus, There is a Reg't of Engineers here
fixing up several old Engines, and repairing cars &c,

June 29th, Morning hot, rain in the evening, wrote some letters.all quiet,

June 30thRegiment Mustered for pay, Again on picket about half mile south
of town at the Forkadeer bridge, Cool breeze this morning,The
town cows cross this bridge going out to pasture in the morning,
and return in the evening, We held up several while we milked
enough for our coffee, Fill a canteen and hang it in the river
over night, It is generally clabber in the morning, Our "toll
is light as we leave the owners the "heft of the milk,
Some of the old women in town are complaining that their cows
are going dry because they eat so much "hard tack" about our
camps, They charge us 25 to 30 cents for a canteen full,So if
we can take "toll" at the bridge we save our money and get some
milk all the same,

July 1st 1862, Came in early this morning to find the Regt gone with the
2oth,45th, and 29th, Our Third Brigade, Raining,

July 2d, Boys came back this morning tired and foot sore, A good many of
them gave out and layed down by the road side unable to go any
further.

July 3d, Battalion drill at 6 o'clock this morning, quiet balance of day,
wrote some letters, weather hot.

July 4th, On guard at Col Marshes Head Quarters, Exeept Col Nevius Officers
-----.

(61)

are-celebrating, raising the " devil"generally, Salute fired at
are Col Nevius' nearest companions,
1 o'clock P M, hot and dust plenty, The Testament and Tactics

July 5th. Relieved from guard duty, Morning quiet,

July 6th. Not very well , Pleasant ,cool.

July 7th. Brigade drill at sun rise, Hot as usual,Health of camp fairly
good. Went out and picked some blackberries mash them in a tin
cup with sugar fine eating this way and also make nice pies,

July 8th. Boys out on Battalion drill, I am on picket.

July 9th. Relieved from picket at 4 A M, had only two hours to stand,
From 10 to 12 midnight, The moon shone bright and the time
passed quite pleasantly. No "Secesh around, Hot as usual,

July 10th. Returned to camp, all quiet nothing going on, No news from
Richmond,

July11th, Companies " B, D, and H, all packed up for a start, Are going
on the cars as soon as they arrive from Corinth, Cars here at
last, And at 4 P M, all aboard, We rode about two hours, Then
Co "D. Was left to guard some bridges, We proceeded on till
we reached a small place called Henderson, Where there are
barracks erected for the accomodation of about 1000 men all
deserted now by the original builders, We took possession,
After supper a detail was made of six men from each Company,
I was one of the six from our Co" B,We marched up the Rail R
and left four men at the first bridge, Then four at the next
bridge, I happened to be with the last four, had to march
nearly five miles before we reached our post at the last bridge
There is a wagon road crossing the R, R, here a very dangerous
and exposed position for a Corpl and three men. five miles
from camp. We bivouaced in the corner of an orchard near the
crossing,A farm house farther up the hill with woods on the
other side,We divided the time ,two stood guard until midnight,
Then the others relieved them and stood from midnight until
morning. Were not disturbed, Our orders are to shoot any man
caught burning bridges or cutting telegraph wires, A Corpl
and three men will be likely to drive away a company of bridge
burners. And they five miles from camp,

July 12th, Day light cool and damp a heavy fog hangs around the brush and
woods, The night passed off without accident or incident, Picked a
cup full of blackberries, with a biscuit made out a comfortable
breakfast, The berries here are very large and plenty. growing wild
along the fences, old logs and the R. R. Relieved about sun down
by four men and have to march back to camp about five miles.

July 13th, Sunday morning clear and fine,All in good spirits, Boys lying
around in the shade,

July 14th, Quiet about camp, Train came in but brought no news. Shall have
to go on picket again, This time for 48 hours, Marched up to the
same bridge ahd took up our station in the orchard again,

July 15th, Night passed quietly no disturbance,

July 16th Yet at the bridge, Succeeded in capturing a chicken, One of the
boys got some potatoes, Will have a good breakfast, Cool,it is
trying to rain a little, Releived at 5 P M, Returned to camp by
the foot route, Had a good supper of fresh pork, tea and bread,
Been troubled with camp dysentery, tea and blackberries helpful,
Fresh pork islnt just the thing, however we eat any thing,
all tastes good to a hungry soldier,
Went to bed, began raining and blowing, finally blowed the tent
down, I crawled out from under the wet canvass got my blankets
went over to the Depot and slept the remainder of the night,

July 17th, Wet and cool raining all the morning.

July 18th, Went out in the country and found some pretty good eating
apples, Returned had supper when the Orderly shouted"Carrington

get ready for picket with 48 hours rations, All right. About
sun down was on my post, Some time in the night was awakened by
a noise like the galloping of horses, We grabbed our muskets
and scattered out under the trees, Expecting to see a squad of

----rebel Cavalry coming down the road, We intending to fire at them and
then hide, Sure enough an old horse had broke loose and came down the
road on the run, We let him pass thinking there might be more, None
came however, All soon quiet. Two took up the watch, And two went to
sleep until the morning dawned.

July 19th. Cool and pleasant morning, We are so few in the Company brings
us on duty often, One day one of our comrades sat down in the
tent door took a revolver all to pieces, laid each piece carfully
down then foll asleep, So we call him sleepy Jake,(Barnhart),
Being with us and spying a chicken he started to run it down,
The owner happened to come across him and observed," I would
like to sell you a chicken",Well!'says Jake "I believe I would
rather buy one than run after 'em this way! So we had chicken
and potatos for dinner,

July 20th, Sunday pleasant, had some apples. On post and relieved late
this evening, returned camp,

July 21st,(Anniversity of Bull Run) Quiet about camp ,wrote some letters.
Henderson Station 18 miles below Jackson. on the Rail Road,
Barracks built here last winter for about 100 men quarters for
the rebels, On bridge guard and picket every two days, On 48
hours at a lick,About 100 yards from my tent I found a large
sweet gum tree, cut off some of the bark, Made a strong tea
of it , has a rather bitter taste but not bad to take is
recommended as a cure for camp dysentery, I find it a great help
in my case,

July 22d, Our time was up Sunday as we drew rations for ten days only,
Not relieved yet, The boys call it Halleck soup, It is
made of all kinds of vegetables that have been dryed and then
pressed in to square cakes, potatos, onions, green beans, cabbage.
lettuce, beets and pumpkins, this last spoiled the whole business,
We break off a chunk put it in the camp kettle and boil with plenty
of water and it makes a very good soup, all except the pumpkin,

July 23d,   Leave Henderson Station for Jackson to day Boys are striking

tents now. Aboard the cars and on to Jackson where we arrived
about noon, marched out to our old camp ground,Back to Jackson.
We had good times down there getting plenty of peaches, apples,
and no end to fresh pork, hen turkeys, geese and chickens. As we

took only 10 days rations we were relieved by another Company.
Our duty rather heavy having to guard bridges and do picket duty
just half the time. especially the wires and bridges at night,
Day time we could roam around ,see the country. Now in Jackson
will have to come down to battalion drills &c, Cant go up town
with out a pass, Patrols on all the streets, Have flour and meal
so now I will make some nice biscuits, blackberry pies, Bake in
ovens already here,
Fred Merriman has just returned to the Company having been
absent sick for some time,

July 24th,   Packed up for a start some where, Left camping place about
11A M, and marched a north course after about 15 miles on the
road bivouac for the night, did not pitch our tents. But laid
down and slept very sound until 3 o'clock in the morning. Got
up cooked breakfast of bacon, tea and hard bread. Then took up
the line of march.Our destination being Lexington the County
seat of the adjoining county where they were trying to raise a
Company of Volunteers for the protection of their (Union)
property from roving bands of Secesh.

July 25th,   Arrived at Lexington just about noon having marched the whole
distance of 28 miles in one day or a little over. Lexington is
a small place, Secesh having all left. There is a strong Union
sentiment. Ladys waved their'kerchiefs at us as we marched by.
Have a cool shady place to camp, Water is not very good, Tired
and dusty so will quit, and rest,

July 26th, Warm as usual, Citizens are flocking in from the country to take the oath, Quite a number have come in and still they come.

July 27th, Sunday pleasant, cool nights and hot days. Divine service, The Regt. fell in and marched to Church without arms, passed off very nicely,

July 28th, Up at 1 o'clock this morning, Had breakfast and ready for marching. Started about 4 A M, and by day light were out of town on the road to Jackson, distant 28 miles; we carried no very heavy load, each man with his haversack, canteen, catridge box and musket, marched until noon then two hours rest. And on the road again, Just this side of Jackson a mile or so was a fine spring of clear cool water, So two or three of us got ahead of the command and pulled out for this spring, We marched hard and fast in order to keep out of sight of the head of colum. We finally reached the spring, bathed our faces and hands, drank of the cool water, then rested in the shade until the other boys came along , took our places in ranks and marched on to Jackson, Reached our old camping place stacked arms just about sun down having marched 31 miles altogether, Boys dropped down and went to sleep; some few pitched their tents, I was too tired, lay down and slept first rate until after sun rise, had breakfast set up tents and suppose we will soon go again,

July 29th, Morning cool, Reported that we are to be attacked here, The rebel Cavalry are to make a dash into the Town, cut us up as much as possible then clear out as fast as they came, They burned a bridge above here on the Mobile & Ohio R.R, Our Cavalry had a skirmish with them , Some killed on both sides. Four men living close to the bridge are to be hung, Burn the houses, fences, stop bridge burning,(Camp talk)

July 30th, There was no alarm last night as was expected, All quiet.

(66)

July 31st,   On picket to day, weather cool. Nothing of interest going on.
        Some talk of the Regt going to Cairo, with our rations we drew
        what they called "desiccated potatos". These are ground up and
        dried so they are about the size of buck shot. The Boys call them
        "desecrated potatos", we dont go much on that kind of grub.
        Bacon is good fryed, but pickled pork is the best, sliced, placed in
        frying pan with water, let it boil, then pour off the water, roll the
        slices in flour (if you happen to have flour), then fry brown and with
        hard tack you have a meal. A

Aug 1st. Relieved from picket at 9 A M. Talking about going to Cairo. Will
        be paid in a day or so,

Aug 2d. Hot as usual, Our pickets were relieved by the 20th Regt. In order
        for us to get ready to go to Cairo. Paid off just at tattoo.
        Being the last Company paid, I received $20,25. Had to settle
        for eleven months clothing account. Some of the boys did not get
        a cent. Some $1. and others less. I did not go in so heavy on
        clothing. After this the boys will not draw so fast on uniforms and
        under clothing; be more careful and not throw away on every march. We
        are allowed $42. per year for clothing at Uncle Sam's prices which by
        the way are very reasonable. Some of the boys are careless about disposing
        of under clothing, rather than carry a heavy knap sack. This will be a
        good lesson for all . A letter from home; enlisting for the war is
        the order of the day,

        The 8th Wis Inftry. Have a live Eagle that they carry on a frame. along
        with the Colors. They carried him through the Battle of Shiloh.

Aug 3d, Sunday, Cool and cloudy, Packing up for a start, Speeches by
Genl McClernard and Genl Logan just before we left, Got our camp
equipage and our selves aboard the cars about noon, Arrived at
Humboldt at 1 P M; Stopped and had dinner, 17 miles from Jackson,
Going up towards the Depot I heard some one call my name in a weak
pipping voice and was much surprised to meet John Collins of our Co
Who had just returned from Hospital, He was very weak, Terribly
pitted in the face so I hardly recognized him. Had a severe spell
of the small pox, How he did "cuss " the South for all his misfort-
-unes; from a strong hearty man, to a puny weak voiced spindling,
We Boarded the train , passed through a swampy country, heavy timber
apparantly unsettled, and reached Columbus just at dark, Left the
train marched aboard the Steamer Tatum, On the Mississipi river and
headed up stream, Arrived at Cairo some after mid night, Slept until
day light this morning,

Aug 4th, Left the Boat and marched out to the Barracks vacated by the 63
-d Regt, Ills Inftry, Will have a good time cleaning up as these
quarters are very dirty, Would rather have stayed in Jackson, It is
much more healthy there than here, Muddy and some like rain,,
Saw Major McGowan of Camargo, Ills, About 100 runaway Negros*
came with us,

Cairo, Our arrival here completes our first Campaign, Via, The cold
rains of Ft Henry, The snows of Ft Donelson, The mud at Shiloh, And
the dust and heat of the movement towards Corinth, to our Company
and Regiment, The experiance and military knowledge gained from
this stand point could hardly compensate for the fearful losses
sustained, Yet we have born the battles and marches with cheer--
ful obedience to our Commanders, And now with more confidence in
each other as Comrades, We are ready for any service for the
Union.

Aug 5th, On guard , Have been bringing in drunk men until the guard house
is about full, Some for 10 days and some for longer terms. Fighting
among them selves, Hot,, temperature is 90' to 100' in the shade,
Our location is opposite the St Charles Hotel and close to the Ft.

Aug 6th, Very warm, The mosquitos are so bad, Can hardly sleep for them,
Have to make a smudge and smoke them out or go to bed late,

Aug 7th, On guard, Orders are very strict, No one allowed out of camp with
    out a pass, Hot,

Aug 8th, Sick with fever and hard head ache, (Musquitoes very bad,)

Aug 9th, Went to the Hospital this morning to get some medicine. Received
    five powders enough to kill most any white man. Boys are cleaning
    and white washing the quarters,

Aug 10th, Some better, Detailed for guard duty, , went aboard tug and steame
    up the Ohio river about three miles to the old steamer Illinois,
        She is tied up on the Ills side and loaded with Amunition,15000
        loaded shells besides barrels of gun powder, They fired a salute
        of 13 guns at the fort, havent' learned what for,(Unless it's my
        Birth day,) Cool and very pleasant up here.   20 years old

Aug 11th, Releived from guard, Returned to Cairo on the tug boat, marched
        to quarters, quiet in camp, Squads of soldiers and police are
        forceing all the idle men about town to work on the Boats loading
        supplies for the fleet down the river off Vicksburg,

Aug 12th, About camp and resting, So few men here we have plenty of guard
        duty,The New Regts! are taking the field and the old ones with
        thinned ranks like ours are doing the guard duty,I would rather be
        in the field.

Aug 13th, On guard up the river on the steamer Ills, The Boat is tied up
        to the bank with a gang plank out, Nice shady place, We make a fire
        on the bank back from the river for cooking our coffee. Have to be
        very careful about fire, no smoking allowed on the Boat, Quiet and
        pleasant here, Boats are passing up and down the river on their
        regular trips,

Aug 14th, Morning on guard, Relieved at 10 A M, Rode down to Cairo on the
        steam tug Restless, Sitting on the stern watching the propeller
        churn up the suds" The little Boat makes quite a fuss but runs
        very fast,

Aug 15th, Off duty to day, Clean up and rest, musquitos sing the same song
        all night nearly, Suppose they get tired about the same time we
        do and go to sleep,

(69)

Aug 16th, This morning finds me on the Boat guard again, Cool and pleasant,
        Fleas and mosquitos in abundance,

Aug 17th, 7 A M on the Boat guard, Relieved at lo A M. And back to camp,

Aug 18th, Had to go on guard again,

Aug 19th, Relieved from guard, It is reported we leave Cairo in a day or so
        Our old mess chests turned up to day, We sent them from Fort
        Donelson six months ago, Seemed like meeting old friends as we
        took out our tin ware, Our mess of six left Birds Point with the
        Reg't the 3d of Febuary, Five out of the six were wounded at the
        battle of Ft Donelson Feb 15th, One of those five was killed at
        Shiloh, the others being Home on furlough escaped the battle of
        Shiloh, Marching orders, Left the Barracks at 9 P M, Aboard the
        Steamer J S Pringle, Headed up the Ohio,

Aug 2oth, Arrived at Paducah some 6o miles up the Ohio. about sun rise,
        Took in coal, also three pieces of artillery. one 6 pdr' and two
        small 2 pdr's on up the river arrived at Smithland a small town,
        A few stores on the levee, besides the fortifycations.After staying
        about two hours the Boat was turned down stream. A few hours more
        brought us back to Paducah, The guns were taken off, then we
        started for Cairo with out a fight, Proceeded some 2o miles when the
        Boat tied up for the night the river being very low,

Aug 21st, About day light started on down the river for Cairo, Where we a
        arrived with out accident about 9 A M, The new Gun Boat Eastport,
        has just come down from Mound City and is Here taking in provisions
        and her crew,

Aug 22d, Back in the old Camp and off for the Boat guard as usual,

Aug 2 3d The Regt' left at 3 o'clock this morning, Going to Ft Donelson.
        The rebels have captured Clarksville Ternn, and taken the 71st Ohio
        prisoners, The rebels made them take the oath not to fight against
        the south until exchanged,

Aug 24th, Sunday, The day has passed quite pleasantly or nearly so as the
        sun is not quite down, I go on guard at 7 P M, We leave in the
        morning for Paducha Ky, To take up our abode there, 1 P M,the 72d
        Ills Inftry arrived on the Steamer City of Cairo.Also 13oo rebel----

--prisoners to be exchanged at Vicksburg Miss,

Aug 25th Relieved from guard this morning by a detail from the 72d Ills,
Packed up our traps and at 1 P M, off for Paducah, Good many of
the bove sick, lo P M. Arrived at Paducah, Slept on the hurricane
roof, Cool and fine,

Aug 26th, Got up before sun rise went ashore and stacked our arms. Then had
the Boat to unload, which we did at short notice, The rest of the
Regt' arrived about sun set,(Layed down for sleep), When orders came
to march with three days rations, Started at lo P M, Marched to
the Boat got aboard and headed up for the Tennessee river,

Aug 27th, Morning finds us on the Tenn river bound for Ft Henry where we arr
arrived just at noon, Marched off the Boat stacked arms and drew two
days rations, Going to march to Clarksville, As the rebels are
reported in force out there,There are four Companys of the Curtis
Horse here also several guns form the Garrison of Ft Henry,

Aug 28th, Appearance of rain, Slept at the root of an old tree without any
blanket,Marching orders, Company "B detailed for rear guard,
Started about sun down, The Regt' with four guns in the advance,
Nine or ten wagons in the rear, Had some hard work helping them
up the hills, Marched till midnight, Made my bed in an old cart
by the road side,slept soundly till the eastern sky was flushed
with the morning light,

Aug 29th, Started on the march a little after sun rise, Very warm and dusty,
Halted for rest about noon in sight of the rifle pits of Ft Donelson,
Stacked arms and began cooking side meat and coffee. Remained
here all night,

Aug 3oth, In camp awaiting orders, Alarmed the camp by the pickets firing
their muskets when relieved from guard this morning. On the sharp
look out for Guerrilas, All quiet now, Afternoon, Shouldered our
muskets and soon at the old camping ground just 4 15 P M,
Dover was burned in a skirmish a few days ago between a part of the
71st Ohio and Col Forrest's Guerrilas, Boys are all in good spirits
and "spilfire" for a fight,

(71)

Aug 31st, Sunday, On fatigue throwing up breast works, Our force here is pa part of the 71dt Ohio, 13th Wis, Inftry. Two guns of Floods Battery, And the old Eleventh, Are looking for the rebels at any moment. Muster for pay at 4 P M,

Sept 1st, Morning clear and pleasant. quiet about, camp,. Went down to the Cumberland river and had quite a nice swim, Col Newius came from Ft Henry with about 40 of the boys that were left sick at Paducah, Afternoon, Several of the boys ,myself included went over to the battle ground and built a fence around the graves of our boys that were killed Feb 15th last, After completeing the fence of poles and brush best we could, walked on over to the farm house that afforded our wounded a shelter at the time of the battle. The house was south of the field in a valley, A fine orchard of peach trees, ripe fruit, We ate some nice peaches, Drank of the water from a fine spring near the house, The Lady told us the smell of gunpowder and blood was yet in the rooms where our wounded had lain, and several died, (It was a sight when we was there the evening of the Battle),

Sept 2d, A squad of 38("we boys) Went over the river and "cramped" all the "roasti'n ears, apples, peaches and water melons we could carry, Took them without "axing" the price of the owners,, P m On guard down at the river to keep the boys from going over on such like expeditions .

Sept 3d, Cool and pleasant, Some of our men went out and confiscated some three or four barrels of whiskey, That accounts for so much noise about camp this morning, For breakfast had fresh pork, hard tack and coffee, On guard at 1o A M. Several of the boys have gone out "jayhawking" took their guns with them for fear of the Guerrilas,

Sept 4th, Clear and cool, Review to day, Col Ransom in Command,

Sept 5th, All packed up and ready for marching, Crossed the Cumberland river at the ford water being low, Started early, marched till noon, Camped at an old Iron Furnace owned by John Bell,(candidate for President,)Had all the chickens green corn, apples and peaches we could eat ,------.

--rected a while then started at 7 P M, marched untill midnight, Laved down and slept till morning,

Sept. 6th, Got up early had breakfast, started at 8 o'clock. Our force consists of the 13th Wis, Inftry. the 11th Ills Inftry and part of the 71st Ohio Inftry,Two sections of Floods Battery, (four guns) And about 600 Cacalry mostly Curtis Horse, Morgan is said to be at Clarksville with a large force, Our Cavalry drove about 200 of the rebelsto with in some three or four miles of Clarksville this afternoon, pickets have gone out, So we will stay here all night. Had a good supper of chicken with the usual amount of hard bread, and coffee, Marched about 8 or 9 miles then camped by a beautiful spring,

Sept. 7th, Sunday. Left our bivouac at 8 A M, Marched with in some four or five miles of the town where we could see the Secesh pickets, Companies "E. I" and "F were deployed as skirmishers,also part of the Cavalry, Soon a few shots passed between them, We now Advanced cautiously, going only a few rods, then halt and form our line. Kept on this way until about three miles of Clarksville.(A negro informed the Colonel the rebels were just ahead of us behind a rail fence),We came up a small hill clear of brush, The road fenced, making a lane, rails flew right and left, We were ordered to the front, Part of the Regt filed off th the left in line, our Company at the extreme left with two guns of Floods battery between our left and the road, The 13th Wis on our left, The 71st Ohio on the right supporting the guns. Cavalry mostly in the rear. Now about 400 yards in advance behind a rail fence that had been doubled, On a cross road at right angles to the road we were on, Were the rebels they intended to give our advance fits as they came up the road,A farm house barn and some sheds to their right, Orchards on both sides of the road, At 11 A M, our artillery opened fire shelling the fence , also sending several shots through the barn roof making the shingles fly, We standing in line watching the artillery men working the guns, (These guns were James' brass Rifled pieces, 6 pounders), and very wicked firers, Some two or three hundred yards off to the left and front

---We noticed some men gather about a large dead oak tree, and motioned
to the gunner near where we I stood, turn and fire at those men over
there pointing in that direction, They sighted the gun and fired
The shot striking the oak about lo feet above ground, And such a
shower of dust, bark, and dead limbs, at the same time five or
six of our boys of Company "E ran away from the tree, They were
on the skirmish line and had collected there for a final dash on
the rebelss behind the barn and fences, We all laughed at them,
It was real funny to see them get away from the falling limbs,
pieces of bark and the cloud of dust that enveloped the tree,
After about an hours shelling the rebels ran away, I saw a squad
of men in shirt sleeves break and run from behind the rail fences,
But stood and looked at them, never fired a shot, I could easily
have hit one with my shoot Enfield, As the artillery ceased firing
we were ordered forward, Formed in line the whole Regt. on the
right side of the road, guns in the lane, Cavalry in the rear,
The band playing "Yankee Doodle" in rear of center behind the
colors, Our bayonets at a charge, through a peach orchard until
we arrived at the fence on the opposite side hill. Then we found
the " Birds had flown", I,E,"Skedaddled ", Gave three cheers not
having lost a single man nor fired a musket, Our shells killed
lo and wounded about 15 of the rebels, A flag of truce came in
for the wounded, But more to see our forces we supposed.
The boys captured 25 horses and mules, all saddled, blankets, also
coats, revolvers, shot guns, rifles and one flag, Two men were
lying near, One with his head shot off, the other both arms and
part of his breast torn out by one shell. Private R------ came riding
a mule with a brass kettle full of honey, Beats the world how
some of the boys can find things, We now advanced in line of
battle towards the town, Arrived the Citizens surrendered the place
The guerrilas left , Retreating in good order as usual. Men were
standing on the street corners with clean shirts on looking at us as
march by that were out at the cross roads to check our advance or
turn us back, Lieut Blackstone of Co ""I was wounded in the leg by
letting his revolver fall, The only one hurt of our command,
We marched in and stacked arms, Detailed guards and pickets, for
the night, ------

(74)

---The citizens (loyal ones of course), Furnished us our supper
of corn bread,biscuits, cold meat &c, we had our own coffee,
Then we layed down for sleep that comes to the tired soldier,
So passed our sabbath,
(The anniversary of Napoleons' battle with the Russians, His Order.
" Given at the Imperial Camp on the hights of Borodino this 7th
of Sept, 1812,")

Sept 8th, Clarksville is a very pretty place on the right bank of the
Cumberland river, Has a population of about 5000 whites,
several churches and a fine College, but empty now, It was occupied
by the 71st Ohio before the surrender, Nearly all the citizens are
rebels, The boys opened a dry goods store and supplied themselves
with pretty much every thing they thought they wanted, Col Ransom
rode his horse in and slashed at some of them with his sabre,
They " skedaddled in a hurry, However he obtained about 300 pounds
of tobacco and divided it out among the boys, Each one had a plug
or more. Got started on our return about 11 A M, Marched 8 miles,
then camped for the night near by a beautiful spring, The spring
bubbled out from the stump of an old tree. and joined a small
stream that flowed over the rocks and on down to the river.
The whole bivouac was startled by a Company of Cavalry charging
down the road with drawn sabres waving above their heads and
yelling like Indians, Boys full of fun, " Many feathers about camp.

Sept 9th, Started early this morning marched along the road until we
arrived at Bells smelting furnace within five miles of Ft Donelson
Camped here, After a full meal of green corn, chicken and coffee,
Several of us started down to the river for a swim, We found a
sunken flat boat, with a track up the steep bank or bluff a small
car used for letting down pig iron,At the top of the bank was a
windlass made for a horse to go round and wind up the chain attached
to the car, So we hooked on the car and by pushing round and round
the car was wound up the bank or high bluff, Then we would let
it go just to see that car go whizzing down the track and jump in
the river, We repeated this several times,It was hard work to get
the car up but lots of fun to see it go down, afterwards had
our swim and returned to camp,------

(75)

        ----Layed down for the night,

Sept 10th   Sun rise found us on the road to Ft Donelson, Where we arrived
about noon all safe,As we waded over the river, The boys fired
off their muskets, several had neglected to take out the
tompion and as a result the muzzles were swelled so the bayonet
would not go on,(Some fileing had to be done later on,)

Sept 11th,Up early and sun rise found us on the march to Ft Henry 12 miles
distant, up hill and down through the woods part of the way,
Reached the Fort at noon, stacked arms and are waiting for a
Boat to take us to Paducah, 4 P M, rain, Had to pitch our tents

Sept 12th, Rain and mud, camp at Ft Henry, Several of the boys myself
included got hold of an old flat boat, Pulled it out in the
river, stripped for a swim, which we enjoyed to the fullest,
diving off the boat, using it as our base of operations,
The Tennessee river is a beautiful stream, clear with sandy
and gravelly bottom, good for fishing and swimming,

Sept 13th, Cool and nice this morning, No Boat as yet. We are about out
of "grub", 6 P M, Parade, 7 P M, Boat in sight,

Sept 14th, Sunday, Warm and pleasant, No Boat to day, 6 P M, Inspection
of arms and equipments.

Sept 15th, 9A M. All aboard the Steamer W L Ewing, Started for Paducah,
11 A M, Fast on a bar 20 miles below Ft Henry. While the Boat is
sparing to get off the sand bar several of us stripped and plunged
in for a swim, After a fine time in the water the boys all got on
board except me *Myself* just as the Boat swung off the bar, The guards were
so high I could not reach, Finally two of the boys reached down
grasped my hands and pulled me up, Dragging me over the boat guards
and landing me safe on deck, My bare breast was considerably
scratched up by this rough operation, At 5 P M further down the
river and tied up for the night,as the river is low, Company "E
detailed for picket duty on shore,

Sept 16th, All aboard , Started at day light. 9 A M, Fast again ,Got off
about noon and no more trouble, plenty of water, Arrived at Paducah
about 2 P M Found the boys that were left behind on account of
      ----

(76)

--sickness, Camped on the river bank near the Marine Hospital,
warm days and cool nights,

Sept 17th,   Camp at Paducah Ky, Rained last night. Cool and damp this A M.
The 72d Regt' left to day for parts unknown,

Sept 18th, Weather fine, Detailed for Provost Guard, Have our quarters at
the"Campbell House "We have a room and fire place,:so when off
duty are very comfortable, The Darkeys to cook and dance for us,
No drill. Our relief has to get up at midnight and patrol the
streets until 6 A M, Then the other relief comes on . We change so
the fore part of the night will be to one relief a week.then the
otheron for the morning turn, Orders to arrest all drunken men,
All soldiers with out a pass, And watch for Secesh" as they are
prowling around here a great deal, And very sly. Smuggling quinhinv
South.We are armed with a revolver and wear a star,

Sept 19th, Dull and quiet about town and camp, Citizens are not allowed to
carry arms or sell whiskey to soldiers,

Sept 20th, Weather pleasant, There was a meeting of Union men in the
Market House last night, Several of the Citizens made speeches,
Our Provo Guard of 12 men is divided into three reliefs of four
men each, On duty four hours and off eight night and day, Our duty
is to look after unruly soldiers and citizens. See that the boys
stay in camp after tattoo, Police the streets during the night,

Sept 24th, Past few days pleasant and quiet about town and camp,
Three Companies of the Regt went away on a Gun Boat up the
Tennessee river,

Sept 25th, The Companies returned last night, No news,
The water in the Tennessee river is very low, But the Captain
of the steamer said he could run his boat"across a meadow if
there was a heavy dew on",

Oct 4th, Quiet up to this date, except the following incident. During this time a young man about 18 years of age, a colored boy but almost white, joined the Company as cook. In the warm afternoon, several of the boys were lying asleep under the shade of a large tree near the tents. This colored boy was asleep lying flat on his stomach with his arms [?]essed under his forehead. One or two of the boys were drilling with an old musket, going through the manual of arms. Tiring of this, he threw the gun down on the ground striking the hammer so it was discharged. The bullet going clean through the colored boy's temples, at the same time cutting through a shoe and taking out one toe of another soldier asleep. The colored boy never moved a muscle, but the dark blood soon formed a pool on either side. None of the boys knew the old musket was loaded, or assumed to know where it came from. We were very sorry for the poor fellow. [?] very long in camp.

Oct 25th, Snow fell today.

Oct 30th, As this detail takes me away from the company and the routine [?]ward is the same thing over and over have made no note of the doings day by day. Our quarters are in the Campbell House rented by the Government Office of Provo Marshall and other offices, &s. The regt left at 8 A M this morning. Took the steamer for up the river, leaving the camp and the sick here.

October 31st, Some of the Cavalry captured a rebel Captain, Lieut and one Sergt some fifteen miles west of town. They were out recruiting for the secesh army. They also confiscated some $4,000 or $5,000 worth of peach brandy and whiskey.

Nov 1st, All quiet. No news from the Regt. Pleasant and warm.

Nov 6th, Last night a prisoner escaped from the guard house. A young man that had been [?] in smuggling revolvers and quinine through the lines to the rebels down in Tennessee.

Nov 7th, The [?] brought in twelve barrels of peach brandy worth $1.50 per gallon. Have been after the escaped prisoner but could get no trace of him.

Nov 11th, The Provo Guards wear belts and carried revolvers instead of our
muskets, I carried an old fashioned pepper box six shooter
revolver,(Allens patent) with it I could do some good shooting
It was very accurate, Some times however the whole six would go
off at once, We are expecting the return of the Regt.

Nov 13th, The Boys came in about 2 P M, They have made a 120 mile march,
But did not catch the rebels.

Nov 17th, 6 P M, The Marine Hospital caught fire and was burned to the
ground. The sick were taken out safely, also about two tons of
gun powder that was stored in the basement, All the equbpments
except part of the beds and cots burned,

Nov 18th, 12 30 A M, We found a woman lying dead down by the river,

supposed to have been murdered, Dark and raining,

Nov 19th,   All quiet around camp and town, Rain and mud,Col Ransom is now
a Brigadeer, The Regt is commanded by Lieut Col Nevius, My Company
is Commanded by Capt H C Vore, 1st Lieut S B Dean, 2d Lieut J D
Vernay, We have nearly a full compliment of line Officers, The
Regt numbers about 250 men, 45 men went to Cairo to be discharged
on account of wounds and disability,

Nov 20th, Leave Paducah to day, down tents pack up and ordered to La Grange
Tenn, Marched down to the river and aboard the Steamer J H Doane,
Got started about 9 A M, While waiting here a little short Irishman
(Barret) of Company "C who had been drinking and bidding friends good bye,
Concluded he could walk around the Boat on the banister of the
hurricane Roof, He started and got along very well until he reached
about the middle on the out side, Here he lost his balance and
pitched head long down into the river, Some of the Boys fished him
out a very wet but possibly a wiser man, Soon after leaving the
Boat got fast on a bar and here we stayed about four hours,
Finally off at 2 P M, and on down the Ohio river,

Nov 21st,   Reached Cairo about 3 P M, After landing at the levee tied up,
Lay here until sun down then backed out into the river, Thence
on down the Mississipi and arrived at Columbus Ky,in the night
about 19 P M,

Nov 22nd, Lay here until about noon. Then left the boat and marched us up to the Soldiers Home. Put us in there and placed a guard around the home. Several of the boys ran away and joined the Regulars.

Nov 23rd, Left Columbus early this morning and arrived at Jackson, Tenn about 3 P M. Stopped long enough to change cars. Then started once more for La Grange. Passed through Boliver, a well fortified place. Arrived at Grand Junction just before dark. Stopped a few moments, then went rolling on, sometimes fast, and sometimes slow. We rode on the top of box cars and could hardly keep our seats as the long train swept around the curves. Many of us sat on the edge with our feet hanging over, but we had to hang on and keep awake. Arrived at La Grange about 9 P M. Was detailed to unload the train, which took us till 1 A M. Then went up to camp and layed down for sleep.

Nov 24th, Marched out about four miles and pitched our tents in an old field. We are now in the 6th Division, Genl Mc Arthur commanding 2nd Brigade on the left wing of Genl Grants Army. This puts me in mind of our advance upon Corinth last spring, with Regts all around us. There is between 50 and 60, 000 camped about La Grange and Grand Junction. They are concentrating for a move farther south.

Nov 25th, Move into the 1st Brigade so that Ransom can take command as Brigadier.

Nov 26th, Weather pleasant. In the afternoon had a division drill of 5 hours duration. Made a fine appearance—long lines of Infantry with batteries of artillery on the flanks, drilling us to make charges in line. Came time to yell like Indians. After parade, wrote letter to Father.

Nov 27th, Pleasant weather. Inspection of arms and equipments. Are to march in the morning with three days rations in our haversacks.

Nov 28th, Left [?] and marched in a southerly direction. Marched all day. Rather a rough country—hilly. Streams and water scarce for so large an army. Yellow clay soil as we march into the State of Mississippi.

Nov 29th, Up and on the road to Holly Springs, skirmishing all the way in the advance. Arrived at Holly Springs about 10 A M. Rested long enough to eat dinner, then started on. Marched seven miles to water and camped for the night in line of battle. Reported one or two killed in advance during the day.

Nov 30th, Sunday, The 11th Ills and 1st Kans Infty with two Parriot guns were sent out to reconnoiter and find the position of the enemy. We took the advance; Kans regt following, artillery in the road, while in the road we advanced at double quick, every mile or so file to the right and form line with the road at right angles. Cavalry skirmishing in advance, we often formed line through brush, tearing down fences, across gardens, passed farm houses, barns, &c. Back in the road and on the run again, canteens and cartridge boxes flopping as we ran. We kept this up for seven miles. Then as we came to the top of the last hill with bottom land along the Tallahatchie River, we saw two forts, one on either side of the road and about a mile away. We now filed by right flank across an open field. I was watching the embrasure when suddenly I saw a puff of white smoke and almost instantly a shell passed over our heads and buried itself in the hill side. Made some of the boys "duck." Our parriot guns took position in a corn field left of the road supported by the Kans Regt and returned the fire. We marched in behind a strip of timber and layed down flat in line. While lying here, a plunging solid shot struck the ground just in front of our Company, throwing dirt over my cape (as we had our overcoats on). Plowed a furrow, raised, passed over my head and struck a hickory tree about ten feet from the ground, going clean through to the rear. This came near taking two or three men out of the ranks of our Co. We lay here about three hours taking their fire. It's hard to lay and be shelled when we can do nothing in return, could see nothing to fire at ourselves. Shell burst in a rail fence just ahead. The pieces hummed towards us but no one was hit.

(We afterwards learned the two brass rifles they used on us here were captured from Dresser's Battery at Shiloh.) Having located the rebels, we lay some three or four hours. As we marched back to the road, Col Ransom flanked the Regt across the open field sloping towards the enemy. The whole Regt in plain view regardless of shot or shell. However, we "ducked" every time one passed, they worked the guns pretty fast, thinking to annihilate us before we could reach shelter. When it comes to firing on a whole regiment marching by the right flank in column of fours across an open field in full view, at less than a mile range and not hit a man must be considered poor artillery practice. Reaching the road we "skedaddled" back to camp. That is we marched by the same road we came and it seemed a long ways as we had been on the run most of the way out (seven miles). It's tiresome lying flat on the ground. Finally Private Bragg stood up adjusted his cartridge box and equipments. With an oath, he said, "Maybe you fellers over there would like to kill some of us." We laughed, heretofore all had been silent in the ranks for we did not know what instant a shell would tear some comrade's life out, and to be buried in such a lonesome spot. We dreaded this, to see a man killed and buried alongside the road then pass on and leave him so. Seemed hard.

Dec 1st, In camp near Waterford, 7 miles from Tallahatchie River. Cool and damp. 4 P M Marching Orders with three days rations. The rebels have evacuated their forts burned the bridge across the river as well as commissary stores. At 6 P M reached the burned bridge and camped for the night.

Dec 2nd, Rain and mud. We advanced this morning, managed to cross the river on the burned timbers, and marched as far as Abbeville. Here we are quartered in the houses of the town, a small town. We found plenty of corn meal, molasses, sugar, and p[?]. Mississippi Central R R station and railroad bridge, large amount of commissary stores also burned.

Nothing like the Government shoe to march in. Generally, men that give out and are found sitting or lying along side of the road have a big pair of boots near by, and blistered feet; The sewed shoe is very easy on ones feet, but when the roads are wet and muddy they slip especially going up hill. So we find the pegged shoe the best. The government sock is also the best. The wool is soft and doesn't cut like cotton. We also wear woolen shirts. They are cooler than cotton and absorb the perspiration. Not so liable to take cold during the weather changes.

Dec 3d, Pleasant this morning mud drying fast,

Prisoners are coming in from below, 4 P M, moved out about a mile
set up our tents and formed camp, _established_

Dec 4th, Pleasant morning, Went out with a detail after forage, got five

loads of corn , killed two sheep and returned to camp all safe,

Afternoon raining but we have our Fremont tent up and a fire

in the stove,which is made of sheet iron like a large funnel with

the big end down, these large round tents accomodate 16 men,

we sleep in a circle with our feet to the center pole,

The old tent leaks badly but am under the blankets, so good night to

all,

Dec 5th, Rained all last night, but at 4 P M the sun is shining,

Out of hard bread but plenty of meat, **We are learning to get our
rations along the road and in the country instead of carring them with
us,**
Dec 6th, Pleasant but cool this morning, Frost last night, have been

out of hard bread for three days now, but for all that I

weighed 170# with my overcoat on, the most I ever weighed, _heaviest_

Dec 7th, Plenty of bread to day, went out in the country some seven or

eight miles after some blacksmith tools which we brought in with us,

The white folks are about all gone South,No body at home but the

negros, plantations going to ruin, fences down and the rails burned

by the Union troops, stock killed and cotton burned and much of it

confiscated,

Dec 8th. Company "B detailed to go out after forage, got plenty of

corn and fodder, weather warm and pleasant, No news of any importance,

Ours the 6th Division is still at Abbeville, The rest of Grants Army

are mostly at Oxford eleven miles below here, recd a letter from sister

Taps are beating and sounding so must go to bed,

Dec 9th,   In camp, Pleasant warm days, Frost at night.

Dec 10th,   Late this evening four Companies of the 20th Ills Inftry,
            came in from Oxford with 800 Prisoners.

Dec 11th,   The 20th Boys stayed with us over night. Had quite a pleasant
            visit as we are old friends, They were in the same Brigade with
            us at Donelson and Shiloh, (Appearance of rain),

Dec 12th.   Camp one mile from Abbeville Miss, Very many of the 800 prisoners
            the 20th Boys brought up are tired of fighting, Want to go north
            Many Germans among them, Our Division is yet at Abbeville,
            Genl Grants Head Quarters are at Oxford 11 miles below, We had the
            advance up to the evacuation of the works at the Tallahatchie,
            Set up our Fremont tent put up the stove with plenty of wood so
            we are very comfortable nights, Our duty is light, One man for
            picket, One for forage, and some times one for fatigue, per day,
            We are allowed only two tents to each Company. We have ten men
            in ours and more in the other. Our Band is "played out", Only two
            drummers and three fifers,The Cornet Band was mustered out at
            Paducah, Under late Order,Band only at Brigade Head Quarters,
            Drummers and fifers to be detailed from the ranks, No more enlist-
            -ment of musicians, A great deal of cotton is being brought in,
            Some marked C S A, Hogs and chickens are scarce the rebels took the
            most of them and we "gobbled" up the rest, We have fresh pork,
            sweet potatos, corn meal, besides our regular rations, The country
            is now stripped of every thing eatible, After burning the depot and
            R R bridge they tried to destroy the commissary stores, But we got
            quite a lot of sugar and molasses, We are 13 days out from Paducah
            Way down in Mississipi.

Dec 13th, 75 Wagons loaded with cotton came in to day, There has been cotton
            confiscated enough to pay for this trip,
            Detailed to work on the Rail Road Bridge,

Dec 14th   Sunday morning, Cloudy but warm, Inspection at 2 P M, Parade
            later as usual, All quiet,

Dec15th, Move to day in another Brigade, Ransom takes command, (2d Brigade)
          Mc Arthurs Division, Mc Arthur is a Scotsman wears a plaid shawl
          wound around his shoulders, and a Scots cap root of the time (Fine
          man, Boys like him), 25 loads of cotton came in,

Dec 16th, Some rain last night, 9 A M, Pleasant and warm,

Dec17th, Detailed to go after forage with 5 wagons and 12 men, went out
          about ten miles, Were to guard the wagons and find anything good
          to eat, Saw a large number of buzzards on dead trees fired several
          shots at them but failed to kill any, They are nearly all wings,
          A hideous looking bird with bald heads and red legs, After loading
          in corn and fodder, (they have a way of stripping the blades off
          the corn stalks, tie up in bundles, makes fine fodder for mules),
          We located an enclosed lot with several fat hogs, A stream of
          water running through, Rump and I cornered up three or four, at
          the same time several were down by the creek, I finally fired at
          one in the corner sideways, intending to shoot him through the
          brain, at the report of my musket, Rump says " you got him", and
          sure enough the bullet had passed through the one I aimed at and
          struck another by the stream and killed both at one shot, We had
          now two fine hogs, Loaded them in the wagon and pulled out for
          camp, Returned all safe saw no Guerrillas,

Dec 18th, Pleasant, Marching Orders, Started at 10 A M, Marched out on the
          Oxford road some seven miles and camped for the night,
          The cars ran to Oxford last night four trains, with prisoners,
          All quiet boys in good spirits,

Dec 19th   We pitch our tents at night and take them down in the morning,
           Roll them up and shove them into the big wagons, the mules haul
           them to the next camping place, if they dont get up we just bivouac
           so we have comfortable sleeping quarters, Started early and
           reached Oxford about 10 A M, Rested a while then marched on and
           camped about 8 miles below town,

Dec 20th, Pitched our tents, Cleaned off the ground, Seemed like we are
          going to establish a permanent camp here,
          (Some talk of leaving in the morning),

Dec 21st, Down tents and off again, Started on the road to Abbeville just
          at day light, Passed through Oxford about noon, And after some
          hard marching reached Abbeville a distance of 18 miles at sun down,
          Back in our old camping place, Pitched tents, had supper and layed
          down for the night, Holly Springs has been taken by Van Dorn the
          cause of our return,

Dec 22d, Up early, down tents, Coffee .hard bread and fat meat for breakfast,
          Fall in , Column of fours and here we go, Tramp, Tramp with 40
          rounds of cat'ridges in the boxes, haver sack and canteen, then on
          top of all knapsack loaded with two grey blankets and short supply
          of under clothing, Overcoat on as the weather is cool enough, Pretty
          good load for a boy to tote 18 to 20 miles per day, Add the musket
          and bayonet 13 pounds more, And here we are, (Uncle Sams first
          75000.) Started at 6 A M, On the road to Holly Springs we met a
          Cavalry Regiment. We kept the road while the Cavalry men rode by on
          each side. Some one asked what Regt! The answer came "11th Ills".
          What Regt' is this, "11th Ills," Then the Boys began to shout, yell
          and hurrah, Col Bob Ingersol's 11th Cavalry. Ills. and we were the
          11th Inftry. First time we ever met,"Three cheers and a Tiger"

          As we go marching by the Colored people of all shades and sizes are
          hanging on the fences watching the Soldiers pass, " Nev'r did see
          so many Yankees", "Whar youn's gwine with yo' sharp stickers on yo'
          guns", "Look way up yonder mo' coming",
          Some sharp replies would come from the line on the fences,
          To questions asked by some "smart Aleck" in the ranks.
          Many of them followed in the rear of the Army,"Wee's free!
          Women carrying babies, besides huge bundles on their head, Men
          boys and girls, Poor things they suffered more than if they had
          stayed on the plantations, Many however remained and took care of "
          "Masters property as best they could, ------

___ Reached Holly Springs at dark, All quiet now, The rebels under
Van Dorn captured the place, Burned part of the town including
thousands of rations, Commissary and Quarter masters stores, The
boys that saw them said they piled blankets and clothing on their
saddles,Besides all the hard bread they could carry away with them
They were too many for the 101st Ills Infbry, also the 2d Ills
Cavalry, They did some shooting however Before they were captured,
The 101st were taken and paroled, The 2d Cavalry lost some men,
part of them got away, but could not save the town,

Dec 23d.   Pitched our tents and suppose we will stay here a few days at
least. all is quiet about camp now,

Dec 24th.   Moved tents inside the Court House square, Quite a handy place
to camp, We are to be Provo Guards, of the town,(Christmas Eve),

Dec 25th.   This is Christmas morning not much like home times, Weather damp
and cool, One Brigade just passed through town on their way to
La Grange Tenn, Grants whole Army is falling back, Grenada has
been burned also Oxford, The Rail Road destroyed up to that place,
we celebrate Christmas with cove oysters, and had a good time,
generally.

Dec 26th, Rain this morning, 300 wagons on the road to Memphis for rations,
We have guards in front of the remaining stores, Some of the boys
myself among the number managed to crawl in the back way of a drug
store, It was partly dark in there, While the boys were searching
for any thing useful in the way of razors, tooth brushes, bottles
of perfume &c &c, I got hold of a cheese box and slamed it into
a glass case making a fearful crash, Enough to alarm the guards
on the side walk, How the boys did get out of there,Our tents
smell like a barber shop,

Dec 27th, Move back into our Brigade to day, Mud and rain, A beautiful time
to move camp but that is the best the 11th can expect,

Dec 28th, The order to move was countermanded, So we continue Provost Guards
for the town of Holly Springs, Miss. A fatigue party is busy
pulling down the walls of the burned buildings,

Dec 29th. Cool and cloudy, All quiet, 10 P M, Marching orders, All packed up
and ready to march. going to Moscow Tenn,

Dec 30th. Started early this morning and marched 16 miles.Pleasant marching
cool and no dust. No water between creeks, yellow clay soil and
hilly. Camped for the night near a stream of water,

Hard Tack, Hard bread or Crackers, What ever the name there is nothin
to compare with it for the bivouac and field, For hard marching it
seems to sustain and keep up ones strenght, To start on a march with
two days rations of soft bread, By night of the first day the bread
would be done for, While on the other hand hard tack can be nibbled
along the road and then have plenty, three make a days ration, CO
One for each meal,(as they are about four inches square.)
Take a little bacon grease and water in a frying pan add one hard
tack,stew over the fire and we soon have a nice mess for breakfast
or dinner as the case may be, A cup of coffee while hot dip in hard
tack and a good meal can be made of this, We like soft bread while
in camp and garrison duty, also corn bread occasionally, But for the
march give me "hard tack", A chunk of fat meat, and a cup of coffee,
Like the Darkeys "possum", Whoopee "go way".

Dec 31st, Reached Moscow about noon, Pitched tents and are formed in our
old Brigade again, Mustered for pay at 4 P M, Six months now due,
We were all standing around our camp fires talking until rather late.
Except some of the older men who being tired had gone to bed,
When some one of Co "I slipped up and threw an old hog skin over the
head of one of our boys, The skin was returned with vengence and
that started it, The old hog skin was passed around pretty lively for
a while,Then more were found as well as sticks, fire brands, any
thing to throw, until the whole camp was in an uproar, Boys yelling
and shouting like Indians,Having a good deal of fun celebrating New
Years Eve, Kept it up until about 10 P M, when Genl Ransom sent
orders for the noise to be stopped,too much of it in camp, Besides
Van Dorn was expected to give us a call with his rebel Cavalry, Might
take a notion to come on New Years night as well as any other,
By mid night or a little after all quiet and settled down for sleep,
(The end of 1862,)

1863

Jany 1st,1863,

Moscow Tenn, A Pleasant frosty morning, Quietly in camp.

Jany 2d, Pleasant, On picket duty, Our train of wagons returned from
Memphis loaded with hard bread and meat,

Jany 3d, Rained all last night, Cool but muddy this morning, Relieved at 8
A M. returned to camp, Raining up to 10 A M,

Jany 4th, Sunday , Pleasant and clear, all quiet, Van Dorn is at Pontotoc
Miss, Concentrating his cavalry, He may give us a call before long,

Jany 5th, Moved our camp nearer the Rail Road, No news all quiet.

Jany 6th, Rained last night Cool and more mud, recd' letters and papers
from home,

Jany 7th, Digging trenches to be prepared for an attack,

Jany 8th, Cloudy and wet, Worked two hours on the breast works,Shovelling
the soil of Tennessee, Other wise quiet about camp,

Jany 9th, Damp as usual heavy fog, Horses have been taken to mount the Regt,

Jany 10th, Pleasant over head but muddy under foot, Marching orders,Strike
tents, Pack up, Got started about noon and marched until we reached
La Fayette just a little before sun down, Pitched our tents,
all comfortable for the night,

ny 11th, Up in the morning early, started before sun rise, We are mostly
out of tobacco, So Powers (Otherwise known as Calamity), and myself
managed to slip out and get ahead of the command, Marching hard and
t in order to keep ahead, There were Block Houses along the Rail
ad, with new Regt's stationed by Companies to guard the road,
T.d' e Boys were out to see us go marching by, This was our chance,
"Bo got any tobacco", Yes! They would hand out a plug, We would
take a bite and pass it on and they rarely if ever got any of it
back,as others were following , We were out of money and tobacco too
While the boys along the road had plenty, And were very liberal,
About 4 P M, We reached Germantown a distance of 16 miles from La
Fayette, Are now only 15 miles from Memphis, The great City, How I
long to see the Mississipi river once more,

Jan 12th,   Broke camp and started early this morning, swinging along
             the road and reached Memphis about 2 P M, set up our Fremont

             tents just outside the City limits, and after marching all

             day I am detailed for camp guard.

Jan 13th   Relieved from guard duty, getting settled in camp, our tents

             are pitched on the blue grass, water handy. *East edge of the City.*

Jan 14th,   Rain, rain, the tent overflowed with water and the mud deep

             enough out side, Paid two months pay $ 26,00. Tom Lewis and

             myself started for the city at dark through the rain and mud,

             looked around, bought some little articles and returned to

             camp.

Jan 15th,   Lasts nights rain turned into snow, and this morning it is

             five or six inches deep and still snowing.

Jan 16th,   Snow and very cold, not clear yet, very comfortable in our

             tents with a stove and good fire, the snow banks up our tent,

             outside keeps out the cold,

Jan 17th,   Clear sun shine, snow stays about the same, something unusual

             for Memphis, We have had a good time , one or two nights at the

             Theater, the whole 6th Division filled the house, with blue

             coats, neither Ladies nor Citizens, all soldiers, with the

             Boys all about sobered down spent their money Soldier like,

Jan 18th,   Marching orders, pulling down our tents left dry circles in

             the snow, Started for the Boat and marched aboard the Steamer

             Superior about 7 oclock, the 11th Ills, 17th Ills and part of
             the 16th Wis, Infty, our Division is on the boats, waiting
             for some boats down the Ohio, river high, drift running,

Jan 19th,   Taking in coal at the mouth of Wolf river, a mile or so above

             Memphis, weather bad , more rain, be glad when they do start
             we are crowed on this boat, I have to sleep on a coal pile.

Jan 20th,   Got the coal aboard then dropped down to the city, good many

             of the Boys in town yet, muddy and wet at the landing,

             Got started at last about 10A M, on down the river and dark

             finds us fifty miles below Memphis tied up to the Arkansas
             side, our quarters   on the boiler deck, any place but a
             coal pile to sleep on,

Jan 21st,   Started at day light and reached Helena about noon,

             Stopped a few moments then started on our journey down the

             river, The country is low only a few feet above the river

             with thick woods and green cane brakes especially on the

             west side, 7 P M, tied up on the Arkansas side,

Jan 22d,   Started at day light as usual. Passed Napoleon about 10 A M.

             no sign of any person being about the town, also passed

(90)

-- beautiful plantations, Small towns, Dark finds the Boat tied up
to the Mississipi shore, The boys set fire to a large white house
also some Negro quarters,

Jany 23d, On our way eably, 5 P M, Some 12 or 15 mile above Vicksburg,,
tied up on the Louisanna side, Shermans and Mc Clernards, troops
are here, Also ours the 6th Division, Waiting for some other Divisions that are coming down the river,

Jany 24th, Damp and foggy, Still tied up ,On the Boat three Regt's of Infty
besides all our camp equipage, Some what crowded,

Jany 25th. Rain and mud, Our Company detailed for picket, at 7 A M,
Relieved late in the afternoon by the 16th Wis,

Jany 26th, Pleasant and warm, Left the Boat and pitched our tents,
Youngs Point, We are camped on the west side of the river , Can
even now hear the boom of the heavy guns as our mortars and gun boats
throw in a shell now and then to stir them up, Our camp is behind
the levee on a large plantation, The owner and his negros are gone .
The fields are grown up with cockle burs, nearly as high as a mans
head, The country is very low and leveed all the way below Helena,
Where there is no plantations heavy cyprus and cane breaks line
the river, Oh! This is a beautiful swamp, The sunny South,
Reported Banks has Port Hudson, Five new rebel gun boats were seen
yesterday below, I expect we'll have a gay time here yet. Rain
and mud since we landed, River raising fast. Dinner time and I'm
never behind for grub.

Jany 27th, The river is very high, Our camps are on low ground behind the
levee in the cotton fields, Boats are tied up and yet here,

Jany 28th, Hard at work on the levee, The river broke through and we are
trying to stop it, The rushing waters dont seem to mind the dumping
of dirt or brush in the crevases, As the ground is lower back
next to the timber, Will soon fill and leave us only a narrow
strip of ground with the levee for camping purposes,

(9e) B

Some prisoners coming in one day and as
they were passing, One of our Boys a kind
of a "Smart Eleck" Sayss."How many men
has Hood got over there any way, A tall

lank,red whiskered Georgian, Answered and
said, "Oh 'bout nuff fer nuther killin'
dun had two killins",

(Refering to the two battles previous to
 the one in which he was taken prisoner,)

Jany 29th, Have checked the water some as our camp is dry ground yet,

Jany 3oth, All quiet about camp,

Jany 31st, Part of the Regt' have gone out on a scout, 2 P M, Can hear
cannon in the direction they have gone, The First Brigade have
marching orders, are on the Boats ready to leave,

Feb 1st, First Brigade left this morning for up the river, Rain and mud,

Feb2d, Heavy cannonading up the Yazoo, Gun Boat fight, P M the Queen of the
West ran the blockade this morning cause of the heavy firing,

Feb 4th

5th & 6th, The usual camp reutine , The river is the most dangerous foe
we have at present,

Feb 7th, The Regt',except Companies "B and "A , Left for up the river
after cattle and forage,

On some occasions while an Officer was riding by the Boys
would call out "Grab a Root", This meant if you are afraid
jump off, grab a root and hang on.

(92)

Feb 8th,

Orders to move on the Boats at a moments warning, Afternoon, moved on board the Steamer Ed Walsh,

Feb 9th, Got started at just 12 minutes before 11 A M, six boats in all containing McArthurs Division, Kept on up the river all night,

Feb 10th, Arrived at a small town called Providence. some 75 or 80 miles from our last camp, Left the Boat about 10 A M, marched out some

three or four miles and camped for the night in a beautiful place on the bank of Lake Providence, Our Company detailed for picket in a cotton field, Some of our men out foraging were fired on by about 300 rebels, several hurt on both sides,

Feb 11th, Releived from picket, returned to camp on some bodys plantation the fisst Brigade are busy cutting the levee to let the river into the Lake, as they think they will find a short channel

to lead to the Yazoo above the rebel batteries. I think it will

work, as the old channel of the river has been there some time,

gone by, weather is pleasant and spring li ke, saw a peach blossom to day, last night we were on picket in a cotton field

some time in the night a lot of darkys were trying to get in

the lines, the sentry called"halt", they did not stop, so he fired into them,"(about a dozen in all),they dropped their

bundles and ran like race horses, the bullet struck a gate post and saved their bacon,In the morning they had a good laugh over it,

Feb 12th, Detailed for picket, wet and muddy, A party went out in the

country and found a large amount of cotton hid in the swamp, one of the boys shot at a cow in the night thought it was a rebel

Feb 13th, Relieved from picket this morning,our rations are hard bread, fat meat and coffee, with beans, and Halleck soup occasionally, candles and soap,

Feb 14th, Our rest day in camp. cleaning up the musket and keeping our cartridge box dry,

Feb 15th, Well here we are on picket at a large steam cotton gin,there

is a large platform built up high off the ground for dyying the

cotton, and stored in the upper floor is a large amount of

cotton in the seed, this makes a fine bed for sleeping while

off guard, standing on the platform we can see all over the level cotton fields, not much danger from guerrillas as the low

ground back is covered with water,so we are between the river and the

swamps, one year ago to day the Battle of Ft Donelson which

we well remember, About midnight I was on out post sitting with

my back to a gate watching the road leading out, when suddenly without a sound to break the stillness a large white dog jumped through the gate close beside me and galloped on up the road, coming from behind,and to say I was startled would be putting

it mild , I soon realized what it was, but before I could

move or shoot he was off down the road and gone.

Feb 16th, Just in from picket on a rainy,wet morning, we have rain one

day for the benefit of the country,in general,the next for our
benefit while on picket, and the next for variety,some of the

boys when they come in from picket in the morning lay down and
go to sleep, I generally clean up and set down and read or

write letters home,then when night comes again Am ready for a

good nights sleep,
      The 2d Brigade has the picket duty to preform, while the 1st.
Brigade does the cutting of cannals, attending the water ways,
while off we read,write, sing songs, tell yarns,and keep the
rations from spoiling, making pipes out of canes, finger rings
out of coal, shells, slate&c, according to the genius of the
soldier,

Feb 17th, More rain, on guard, went to sleep nice and dry, about day

light in the morning water was seven or eight inches deep in
the tent , blanket all wet had to stand up till day ,
got some plank and rails and made a floor in the tent, ready
for the next flood,

Feb 18th, Camp quiet and drying,

Feb 19th, Sun came up clear and warm this morning,

Feb 20th, Pleasant and warm , sun shining,and mud drying,about time for

the spring rains to be over, No movement towards Vicksburg

as yet, The Officers are very strict, have five roll calls
per day, also camp guard, cannot out of camp, have to have a
pass signed with red ink, All comes on account of some two or
three getting out and plundering the citizens, verry nice,

Feb 21st, Clear and warm, mud drying up fast, On picket,

Feb 22d, Relieved from picket, pleasant and warm,

Feb 23d, Logans Division arrived, First Brigade consisting of the 20th,

124th,31st, and the 45th Ills, one of the 2d Ills Batteries,
camped half mile up the Lake from our camp,

Feb 24th, Went down to the river, they are moving a tug from the river
into the Lake, slidding it on timbers over land.

Feb 25th, Raining again, mud is deep and nothing but mud,

Feb 26th, & 27th, Quietly in camp,

Feb 28th, Warm and cloudy, muster for pay, inspection of arms and
equipments,

March 1st, Sunday morning, pleasant and warm,Inspection of quarters,

at 2 P M, nothing of interest going on,

March 2d,On camp guard, Company "G all in the guard house, or in the

absence of a house,are under guard, for refusing to serve under

(94)

a newly appointed Lieut', Sergt Major, Blake was appointed 2d Lieut
to take command in Co "G", the boys stacked arms, swore they would
have their own Lieut's or none, most of the Regt sympathize with
them, Blake was formally a Sergt of Co "D, Genl Ransom came down
and talked with them but no use, they are still under guard,
Blake had been a clown or connected some way with a circus,
while we all liked him well enough, the boys thought they had
material in the Co for Lieuts, He would sing to the Bugle notes,
"Where, oh where, is Seigle, back in the rear with the Artilleree",

March 3dm Pleasant and warm, Had a battalion drill, Parade, as usual.

Cleaning up quarters arms and equipments,

March 4th, Warm as usual, Inspection at 2 P M, of arms, equipments and

quarters, $ 10.00 is up for the Co" that has the cleanest arms

and equipments, $5,00 for the best looking quarters, tents,

parade grounds&c, (The steam tug is in the Lake,)

March 5th, On guard,

March 6th, Raining again, relieved from guard this mornong, all quiet,

March 7th, Detailed for picket, gather up musket, gnub, and go,

March 8th, Relieved from picket this morning, cloudy but no rain,

March 9th, The health of thecamp is fairly good. only a few sick in our C$

March 10th, Rain and mud, Pay/d two months pay. $ 26,00.

March 11th, Pleasant and warm, On fatigue duty to get wood for cooking,
water all over the country,

March 12th, Clear , beautiful warm morning, /All quiet about camp.
no news, recd a letter from home,

March 13th, Fine weather, water is rising rapidly, if it keeps on our
camp will be flooded, nothing unusual about camp, Grant's
Army laying along the river, north and west of Vicksburg,
Working on that canal which I dont think will amount to
much, Our canal here is doing well , some 3000r 400 negres
working daily,, we have a Gun Boat in Bayou Mason,

March 14thm, Pleasant, ground is hard and dry once more, Our quarters
look clean and comfortable; Prize drill to day, $5,00 for
the best drilled Company, Afternoon, Companys "A and "C
got the five each, no difference in their drilling,
grass is green, flowers in bloom,

March 15th,
Sunday and raining, one Brigade of Logans
Division marched down to the boat at 5 P M, and started up
the river, sun shining, no danger of the rebels attacking
us here as the water is all around, with the exception of
a strip of ground along the levee,

March 16th, Warm and nice this morning, 6 P M, marching orders,
left our camp in charge of the sick and a few men to take
care of tents &c, got ourselves aboard the steamer Chanceler
At a little after dark 9 P M, Started at about 10 P M, run
all night,

March 17th, Arrived at our destination, Great American Bend, or "Shirt
Tail Bend" Soon after sun rise landed at Worthington's

Landing, left the boat and marched out about six miles after cotton, loaded our wagons and returned without seeing any rebels, On guard,

March 18th, Pleasant and warm, marched out about four miles after cattle,

get only a few very poor ones at that,Col sent just 20 of us out to skirmish through the woods , ahead of the others,

We found nothing but cane breaks and mud holes, (Nary a Secesh) returned a little before sun down,

March 19th, On guard, Hauling in cotton,afternoon the Steamer Empress came up with 43 wagons to bring in the cotton,There is several

thousand bales hid in the woods,and swamps,all marked C.S.A, the bales are covered with gunny sacking, bound down with bands of hoop iron and hickory withs.

March 20th, Weather fine, cotton comes in, Lieut Vernay of our Co went

out with a party and brought in 195 head of beef cattle,

March 21st, Marching orders, Companys "B "C and "F started about 4 P M, marched through the woods and cane breaks, reached a bayou

which we had to cross in canoes and skiffs, marched in all about 7 or 8 miles until we came to a cotton pile under a shed,

I was detailed for picket, the others went to work and built up a fort of the cotton bales, some two or three bales high,

March 22d, Relieved from picket , had breakfast of hard bread, coffee, and chicken, we have near one hundred chickens tied up ready for our Yankee appetites, A party went out to look for more cotton, found where a pile of about a thousand bales had been burned, it is nearly all marked "C S A, we are on a farm or plantation that Stephen A Douglass used to own, and does yet for all we know, a good many of

his darkeys are here yet, they say it is a long while since they saw him, Afternoon, Heavy firing off towards Yazoo and Vicksburg,

March 23d, Morning rain and mud, the shed and cotton makes us a very good shelter as well as protection in case of a fight, the Bayou runs close to the cotton fort so cant cross unless we swim, On guard, about noon one of our Co swam the Bayou and out some two or three miles captured four horses, led one and rode the other and so got across the Bayou, all right, and returned to camp,afternoon sun shining pleasant .

March 24th, Some rain before noon , clear this afternoon, On picket to night,Stenger, Col Corpl captured two men, one named Buford the other Crow, they was armed with a knife revolver and double barrel shot gun, said they were out hunting bears,

March 25th, Relieved from picket this morning, pleasant again, some of the boys visited the Douglas plantation house, they are hiding horses and stock in the swamps,a good safe place,I stay pretty close to the fort, likely to be rebels in the woods and might pick a straggler up,

March 26th, Pleasant , Orders to return to the river and leave this cotton,cant get the wagons out here on account of Bayou Granicus to cross,and muddy roads, got started about noon , and arrived at our first camp on the river some time before sun down,

Woods

Cotton fort Sheet

cotton bales

C.S.A.

Douglas Plantation

Swan Bayou

March 23d, 1863,

woman
At the Douglas plantation Lyons bought a rooster of an old colored
for 25cents, that he named "Old Dog." He carried this rooster on

his knap sack , while marching until after the seige of Vicksburg,

When he finally took him home. During the seige the boys could

hear a rooster crow and wondered how one could survive.

(96)

March 27th, Cloudy,appearance of rain, detailed for guard,
        (Steamer Empress,

March 28th,   All aboard,and leave for our camp down the river,

            Started at lo A M ,   And on down the river and at 4 P M,

                landed but remain on the Boat,Our camp has been moved

            six miles up the river, the boys had to move camp several

            times on account of high water,The levee was cut the day we
            left Providence, now it is water where our camp was,

            Found our camp equipage aboard the Tatum,got my knapsack
            was afraid it was lost, all my valuables were in it,

            Finally landed after dark three miles below Providence,
            on a small patch of dry ground, slept on the Boat.
            The wind blew awful all night was fearful the boat would
            be swamped,

March 29th,   Left the Boat and pitched our tents in front of a

            large white house belonging to some planter,And here we are

            in our old Fremont tent, the wind blowing cold outside,
            we have a good fire inside and the smoke goes up and down,
            every way but out at a small hole in the top of the old tent,

March 30th,   Cold wind blowing this morning, Several Boats loaded
            with troops passed going up the river,water from the levee
            being cut is drowning out the lower camps,every day some of
the Regts have to move to find new camping ground above water,
            Regts and Batteries of artillery with their horses are now
            on the levees, temporarily until they can be moved to
            better camping places, The talk in our camp is that we will
            soon go up to the Yazoo Pass, probably in a few days,
            The lo9thIlls Inftry, arrived in our Brigade to take the
            place of the 14 th Wis who have gone up the river to
            Arkansas after beef cattle,

March 31st, Well here is the last day of march, pleasant morning,
            sun shines once more,Several of the boys are getting ready
            for picket, soon be my turn again, detailed to go after
            forage, got six loads of corn, 5 P M parade,

April 1st, Morning pleasant and warm, some of Co "E boys have a fiddle

            in the next tent to ours and they keep it a goingf from

            morning until night the same tune over and over,Boats pass
            up and down the river loaded with troops and commissary
            stores, warm, Drew new tents , the wedge tent,each tent will
            accomodate four men, have to leave our old ones,like parting
            with old friends, We have six of these tents for the Co,
            four men in each tent, Tattoo done beat,so must to bed as
            all is quiet about camp, except that everlasting old fiddle,
            good night,

April 2d,   A beautiful morning, Guard mounting, the drums sound

            pleasantly, Our friends up North must surely have opened
            their hearts, for we have one potato and three eggs for
            breakfast to the man,sent by them for the Soldiers, "Bravo,

April 3d, Morning pleasant as usual. Two hours drill in the morning,
    Battalion drill in afternoon, Signed the pay roll for four months
    pay, Two Gun Boats and five amunition Boats passed going up the
    river,

April 4th, My time for camp guard to day, paid off this afternoon, My four
    months pay is just $52,oo in bran new greenbacks, lots of money in
    camp, We some times get sheets of 5 cent and 1o cents, ten and
    twenty in a sheet, cut these apart and have our Shin plasters! as
    they are called,

April 5th, Sunday , Beautiful quiet day in camp, Mess No 5 Corpl Lewis,
    Corpl Carrington, Sergt Peck, and Corpl Morris, Black Bill Cook.
April 6th, Anniversary of Shiloh, Wrote letters home,

April 7th, Warm, Sent home my $52. by Mr Johnson of Lacon Ills, He to expres
    it on arriveng at Cairo, Our Officers are getting very strict
    with us all of a sudden, have five roll calls per day, and a camp
    guard, have to have a pass signed by the Col Commanding, with red
    ink, all comes on account of some few of the boys getting out
    and plundering a house, several quilts or blankets were stolen,
    One court Marshalled and sent to the Dry Tortugas for three
    years with ball and chain attached to his leg,

April 8th, Hot and dry, Our Division assembled before Ransom's Head Quarters
    to hear Ajt Genl Thomas speak. He made a short speech in regard to
    Contrabands "Negros", Arming them &c &c, Two Regt's are to be
    raised here and the Officers chosen out of this division,
    (Mc Arthurs), He also spoke a few words and several other of the
    Officers, All were received with great applause,
April 9th, Warm, Nothing but the every day duty of camp life,
April 1oth, Warm and clear, Muster at 1o A M, Not well to day excused from
    duty by the surgeon, The Co in one mess two Negros doing the
    cooking, John D Jvohs Overseer,

April 11th, Heavy firing down the river at entervals. It is reported here
    that the rebels at Vicksburg were fighting among themselves,
    6 P M, Raining the first since we landed here, The raising of
    Negro Regt's goes on bravely. One nearly full already, only two
    days, "Bully for the Darkey Regt's. Its fun to see the black Boys
    get their cat'ridge boxes on upside down, They dont know a belt

(98)

---from a hole in the ground. But seem very willing to learn,
It will be rather dangerous near,when they get hold of a musket
and bayonet Sergt Warren Peck Promoted Captains and is organizeing
a Company of these Colered men,He has to manage them like children
as they are always wanting some thing.

April 12th, Some rain last night, Afternoon pleasant,

April 13th, More rain, Cool, Some firing down the river, Morters sending in
a shell now and then,

April 14th, Dull and wet, Expecting orders to start for Vicksburg,
Reported Charleston S C, is taken,

April 15th, Pleasant and warm, Fourteen Boats loaded with troops passed
going down towards Vicksburg,

April 16th, Health of the camp is good not much sickness,
Brigade drill this afternoon, Eight Boats loaded with troops
just went down, 9 P M heavy firing down the river, feel the jar
in our tents 60 miles above Vicksburg,

April 17th, Had a grand review to day of the whole Division, 1st 2d and
3d Brigades. We had great praise for good marching,
Boats continue to pass going down,
Six Gun Boats and four transports ran the blockade last night,or
passed the Batteries at Vicksburg, Cause of the cannonading
from 9 P M, untill 11 P M , Grants Army is getting below the
City, Clear and warm, Wrote letter home,

April 18th,   Another review to day, Passed off beautifully, Reported the
Boats that ran the Batteries only lost one man,through all that
heavy fireing, 6 P M Rain with some thunder,

April 19th, Wet and muddy, Detailed for picket,"Get yer gun' and here we go,

April 2oth, Morning and just relieved from picket, Marching orders,
      Down tents, and all hands go aboard the steamer Minnehaha, Started
      after dark and arrived at Millikins Bend about 11P M. Remained
      on board all night,

April 21st, Got off the Boat and marched out about a mile and a half,
      Pitched our tents in a large corn field, Appearance of rain,
      Had to put on a camp guard to keep the Boys from Volunteering
      to run the batteries at Vicksburg,Logans Head Quarters was the
      place to get the chance to go , and so many wanted to take the
      chance, (On the night of the 16th the old Steamer Henry Clay was
      set on fire while running past the Batteries of Vicksburg.
      The same old Boat we came down on from Minneseta in the fall of ,
      186o.)

April 22d, Great excitement among the Boys, So many anxious to go on the
      Boats that are preparing to run the Batteries, They want to handle
      the Boats, River men and there is plenty of them in ours and Logan
      Divisions. Those that get through safe are promised a furlough of
      3o days, Gov Yates of Ills is expected to visit our Camp,
      1o P M heavy firing down the river.

April 23d, Seven Boats ran the blockade last night, Our 2d Lieut Vernay
      went down in command of the Steamer Horizon,Stood on the Hurricane
      deck and went through that storm of shot and shell all right,

April 24th, Very warm, The 1o9th Ills Inftry, Consolidated with the 11th.
      One Company "F" comes in entire, Officers and all, the other
      Officers resign, The men come in as recruits filling up the Regt',
      to about 8oo men. We have been so reduced in numbers was afraid
      we should loose our number,

April 25th, Doing guard duty, Col Ransom has received his comm'ssion as
      Brigadier Genl of the 2d Brigade, MCArthurs Division, 17th Corps.
      The boys think lots of Ransom.We are drilling and getting along
      first rate with the"new boys"as the 1o9th boys are called,

April 26th, Marching orders, Left our camp about noon and marched some 8 or
      9 miles,, Stopped for the night in some old plantation houses,
      Found ab old bedstead on which I----- old plantation houses,

List of names transfered as recruits from the 109th Ills Inftry.
To the 11th Ills Inftry, Assigned to Co B 11th Ills Inftry.
April 23d 1863. At Lake Providence La.

Privates.
1   Anderson.Richard
2   Brown.Jesse M
3   Brown.John F
4   Brown.Charles C
5   Brown.George F
6   Brown.David
7   Barnett.Leonard C
8   Barnett.Felix W
9   Barringer.Willis
10 Barringer.Crawford
11 Coleman.Robert J
12 Cochran.William J
13 Crowder.John R
14 Dupass. William (Buck)
15 Edmonds.Allen G
16 Edmonds. Thomas J
17 Edmonds. Jacob K P
18 Felkins. Thomas
19 Fox. Barney
20 Hill.Alfred
21 Johnson. Jeremiah
22 Jackson.Jessee
23 Jones. Amos G
24 Lence. Abraham J
25 Lynn. Jonathan J
26 Lyon.George W
27 Moyer.John M
28 Moore.Henry
29 Montgomery.Joseph M
30 Murphy.Columbus C
31 Manus.James
32 Manus. Tilman
33 Norris.Peter
34 Pate. Charles S
35 Prior.John
36 Prior. William
37 Roach. William W
38 Roach.James A
39 Rhodes. Robert
40 Spire. John
41 Stennett. Francis M
42 Swicegood. Francis C
43 Stamps.John
44 Simmerman. James
45 Thomason.Francis M
46 Thomason.Pleasant M
47 Wilson. George W
48 Wilson.William C
49 Wilson. James
50 Williams. Joseph H
51 Williams. Andrew J
52 Wilson. Joseph H
53 Watkins. Josephus
54 Worbus. Charles

Privates.
55 White. Charles A
56 Windland. James
57 Young. James R
----
58 Bennington.Robert. Recruit,
59 Linscott. Abraham. "   "
                          Of .63

Total of 59 men'.

----slept soundly, Ate breakfast in the same room with two or three
dead cats lying under the bed,

April 27th, Detailed to go back after three wagons, About half a mile
from camp found two of the wagons with the tongues broken out,
cut some poles and soon made new tongues, helped the teamster
hitch up his mules and get them started for camp, Then we marched
back on the road looking for the other wagon, found it at the
river some 8 or 9 miles from camp,tongue broken also, finally
repaired and about 1 o'clock P M, Started and arrived at camp 6 P M
here we found the Regt had moved on, Half mile farther on w , or
the wagon stuck fast in the mud, Took lodgings in an old cotton
gin for the night.

April 28th, Had to leave part of the load. Three of us remained to guard,
While the rest went on after the Regt to a small town called
Richmond about two miles from here, They to send a wagon back after
us,

April 29th, Fighting at Grand Gulf about 30 miles below Richmond, No news
from the Regt. 11A M, Suppose they have gone on , No wagon yet,

April 30th, All quiet no news from below. 1 P M, Wagon comes for us and
the tents)&c that were left, Started and arrived at Richmond
about 3 P M,

May 1st,   Started with the train of wagons for camp, stopped for the night
four miles beyond Richmond,

May 2d,   Got an early start this morning and arrived at camp with out
accident about 1 P M. Found the Company all right, rec'd a letter
from Father,

May 3d, Pleasant and very warm,Inspection at 10 A M, Grand Gulf taken with
a loss of 500 men killed and wounded so reported.

May 4th, Hot this morning, Genl Steels Division passed going down to
Carthage, Plenty of fighting may soon be expected, Tuttles Division
passed at 6 P M, Having some friends in these Regt's We ask "what
Regt is that", "Same old Regt only we got new clothes", And again
" This is Our Regt", Or we'r Co "Q", Is about all one could find
out, Except now and then some older man would answer correctly.
Ills,Ind,Iowa, Mo and other States represented ---

---by these passing Regiments,

As these big Divisions go marching by with rattling equipments,
The long steady swing, The wave of bright musket barrels,

At a "Right shoulder shift", The blanket roll,the knapsack,
haversack and canteen, The car'ridge box, cap box, and bayonet
scabbard all strung on the waist belt, 40 ounces of leaden bullets
with the powder and bullet wrapped in paper to form the cat'ridge,
A hand full of caps, Is the load each man has to carry, Three
days rations add to the weight, But the most of these men are
 strong hearty fellows, Hardened by the service of the past one or
two years as the case may be, We notice their faces, Some look
tired.Some gay and careless, others sober as they realize what all
this means, Then the jolly joker keeping a whole Regt in good
cheer, So they go , many of these stalwart forms will meet a
 soldiers fate in the coming days all toosoon, Then comes the
Artillery with their horses and caissons,Six great horses to each
gun, Six to eight horses to haul the heavy leaded ammunition chests.

Then following squadrons of Cavalry, The gay troopers think they
can ride while we have to walk. But we have no horses to take care
of, When the bullets are singing it is better to be close to the
ground, 450 Rebel prisoners taken at Grand Gulf are camped near,

May 5th, Warm as usual, More prisoners taken and coming in.

May 6th, Battalion drill at 2 P M, A soldier found a small box of jewelry
        buried in the ground near Ransoms' Head Quarters.

May 7th. Cool and windy this morning. About 150 Rebel prisoners passed
        "going north for their health"as some of them expressed it,
        On guard duty,

May 8th, Remain in camp at Smith.s plantation. Near Bayou Vidal, We are now
        below Vicksburg on the west side of the river,

May 9th, Very warm, Roads are getting better, letter from home.

May 10th, Broke camp and about 1 P M, Started on the march, The road is quite
        sandy, We follow the Bayou around towards the south, Marched to
        Perkins Landing about 9 miles below Carthage. On the river once
        more.

May 11th,   Out on the road about sun rise and marched six miles, Stopped

for an hour or so at A C Bowies plantation. (Of Bowie knife fame)

His house was burned to the ground,other houses on plantations also

burned by the advanced Divisions, This house had (so reported)

$40,000 worth of fine furniture, Four rose wood pianos, Three burned.

One was out on the lawn and a soldier playing as we came up.raining

at the time, As the boys passed would hit the keys with the butt

of a musket,and the poor piano responded by shrieks and groans,

Allowed the darkeys to carry off any pieces of furniture they might

select while the house was burning, Negro quarters undisturbed,

I noticed small patches of ground fenced with very high fences,

We learned this was done to keep little "nigs" from being caught

by alligators, We are marching around Lake St Joseph, Saw my first

alligator, It had been killed and layed across the road so we had

to step over it as we came marching along, Guess the cannon wheels

will cut its head off when they come along (smells fishy,)

Several are to be seen on the opposite side of the lake, Boys shot

at one swimming in the Bayou did not kill it, only the hump of the

eye and snout are visible while they are swimming, Leave a long

wake in the water, (The one in the road was about 8 feet long),

They like to lay in the sun on old logs so they can slip into the

water at the first alarm, Orders to follow file leader and keep

in ranks, I noticed Tom Lewis was inclined to follow me even if I

left the ranks, We were marching in a sandy road, looking back Tom

was most industrously shoveling about a spoon full of sand into

the back of my shoes, The toes of his shoes turned up just enough

to enable him to do this, I enquired why he was doing so, " Said

he had orders to follow his file leader". I threatened to march

down in the lake. but I knew he would wait for me to come out,

Marched about four miles farther on and camped for the night,

(1o3)

May 12th, Up early , gathered around the fires, boil coffee, fry bacon,
  and munch hard tack, Sun rise finds us on the road, After marching
  9 miles we reached Hard Times, Went aboard the Steamer Forest Queen
  Run down five miles to Grand Gulf, Left the Boat and bivouac for
  the night, The Steamers here shew the effects of running the
  Vicksburg batteries, 1o inch holes through the Pilot house, Upper
  works damaged in a similar way, There was two Pilets to each wheel
  a 1o inch shot passed through taking out the spokes of the wheel
  and cutting in two one of the Pilets, The other pushed away the upper
  part of the body obstructing the wheel with his foot and held the ^slowly^
  Boat on her course down the river, Only two ^Boats^ of the seven could turn
  a wheel after they got below the Warrenton batteries, They are

  repaired sufficiently to ferry the Regt.s across the big river,
  Saw some big guns in the water batteries, They are just pens dug in
  the bluff low down on the river, The guns in these could hardly be
  hit by the gunners on the Gun Boats,

May 13th, Stayed at Grand Gulf all night, Our tents are all on the other
  side, Have to bivouac now, Started early this morning and marched
  some 8 or 1o miles east and north, Hot and dusty, water scarce, On
  the Willow Springs road, Heat and dust awful, While marching in a
  lane with rail fences staked and ridered on each side I was nearly
  over come and just ready to fall in ranks when the bugle sounded
  halt, I scrambled over the fence took off my cap loosened up my
  equipments, While the boys brought a canteen of water, Resting in the
  shade of the magnolias that were in bloom, I soon recovered.
  When the bugle again sounded the forward, took my place in ranks all
   right, (The nearest I ever came to giving out on the march,)
  The yellow dust was nearly four inches deep as the other Divisions
  had marched ahead of our Brigade, With Artillery and Cavalry,besides
  wagons and all that goes to make up an Army on the march. The dust
  would hang on the eye brows, hair, moustache, settle all over our
  uniforms and equipments. Faces streaked with perspiration until we
  were a hard looking out fit. Some of the boys tie strings around the
  trowsers legs at the ankle, This keeps the dust out but also keeps the
  air out, Much cooler to hang loose, After a days march to bathe the
  feet and ankles is very refreshing, Especially when we can find a
     stream to wash in,

(104)

May 14th, Rained last night, Pleasant marching, Afternoon hard rain making

the roads muddy and slippery for the Infantry as well as for the
Artillery. Warm. Marched 15 miles on the road to Jackson Miss,

Genl Ransom reported Richmond taken, Logans Division had a fight out

on the Black River, The 20th Ills was badly cut up their Col killed,

They drove the Rebels and are on the road to Jackson. At dark we are

in bivouac, The camp fires, The soldiers cooking their evening rations,

The great artillery horses with the parked cannon, The long line of

stacked muskets, The colors cased and lying between the bayonets

glimering in the fire light, We wrap our blankets around our tired

bodies and lie down to rest and sleep.

May 15th. After breakfast we buckle on belts sling on knapsacks haversack and

canteen, "Fall in, Take arms," "Right face," "Right shoulder shift arms"

"Forward march and on the road again, Ransom's Brigade is rear guard

to day, Passed through Utica about noon, Only a small town, Reported

Jackson ts captured, After a pleasant days march of about 18 miles

bivouaced for the night eight miles from Raymond,

May 16th, On the road early this morning, Passed over the battle ground about

bullet scared trees & brush

a mile west of town, Broken equipments, and graves tell the story,

Reached Raymond at 10 A M. Rested until noon, Then started for the

advance six miles out, We can hear cannon and musketry off toward the

north and west, Marched on till we came to the forks of the road, Here

we halted, resting along the road, sitting on the dead leaves in the

shade of brush and trees. The righthand road leads to Bolton Station,
The left to the battle field, All the time we can hear the firing of
cannon and musketry, Ransom wild to get in with his Brigade ,we know
they are having it hot and heavy up there, McClernards four Divisions
just ahead on two roads to our left, Finally the word came to march,
Forward to the Jackson road then turned west , The firing died away
and we reached the battle ground "Champion's Hill" near sun set, The
fight was over the enemy gone, As we marched over the ridge our dead
had been already gathered and placed in long rows ready for burial,
The Indiana Boys suffered severely, On the opposite side of this ridge
road in a ravine lay a great number of the rebel dead, Mostly Georgia
troops, They had worn large white hats many of these were lying on the
ground with bullet holes through them showing the deadly fire of our
men, the position being such that nearly all were shot in the head,
I noticed when the brain is pierced by a bullet the body stiffens in
the position the soldier occupied when struck, If at a charge the
hands and arms remain so, He may drop the musket, or if in the act of
loading the right arm will be extended or raised, These men were fireing over the ridge to hold the road and of course if hit at all the
head being the only part exposed would catch the flying bullets, As we
passed some of the Orderly Sergts were calling the roll of their
respective Companies, We noted the long pauses between names that
answered "Here," and realized that the poor fellows were silent for
ever more, Broken arms and equipments, Splintered saplings and trees,
Blackened muzzles of brass cannon, The dead and wounded, with the --

sickening smell of blood and gunpowder, Groups of soldiers around
the bivouac fires talking over the events of the day,some boastful
others say as they think of the dead and wounded comrades who will
march and bivouac with them no more,The dead were buried where they
fell,both the Blue and Grey, Wounded cared for as fast as possible,
There was more or less skirmishing early in the day getting position
and range, The Secesh had about 20 000 while our forces engaged were
about 9000 to 15000. In the most deadly part of the fight the 8th Ill
charged on the 4th and 6th Georgia,They stood the charge and crossed
bayonets, The 6th Georgia finally broke. The 124th Ills made a splendid charge keeping a line as on Battalion drill, The rebels could not
stand it but broke and fled,This 125th Regt we call them the "One
hundred and two dozenBoys",They captured a six gun battery and many
prisoners,The Warrenton battery of four rifled pieces is among the
spoil of war.
           Leaving the battle field we marched on down the road towards Bakers
creek,the cannon wheels rattling on ahead pf us, many of the rebel
dead were in the ditches on each side out of the way of moving wagons,
guns,and caissions.Near a spring the Boys found quite a pile of pictures
and trinkets taken from the pockets of the Confederate dead,One of the
Boys brought to me a picture of some "Mother in Isreal" Who will wait
and mournfor the son who will never return, On the hill we could see
over the tree tops a solid mass on the Black River bottoms. Reported
that Lorings (Rebel) Division was cut off from crossing the River and
was some where off south offus in the woods lost. We did'ent care to
find them, The Boys of Hoveys and Logans Divisions did the most of
the fighting, Fought all the afternoon hard , We lying in easy suppo-
--rting distance and could have helped just as well as not but no orders
came to move up, Another victory for Grants Army. Pemberton was in
(## note)   Command of the rebel forces,
            Bivouaced for the night not far from Bakers Creek west of the
battle ground,(Called the Battle of Champion's Hill).

May 17th, Our advance this morning captured more Prisoners and 30 pieces of

       artillery, Drove the enemy across Black River, We moved out and reach-
       ed the river to find the bridges burned, Details were made to build a

       bridge over the river, An old cotton gin and other buildings were torn
       down for timbers and boards, They would hitch a rope to a corner post,

       A hundred men grasp the rope while an Officer with a "Heo Heave" with
       a strong pull and out it would come.The timbers laid across, the
       boards for road way, The bridge was fastened to trees on either side

       that had been chopped and fallen in the stream still fast to the stump
       Genl Ransom engineered the whole thing, Men with shovels dug down the

       bank to make the approaches sloping sufficient for artillery and

       wagons to pass, We worked until about midnight,---

Note) Genl Grants Book page 519, The most pathetic sentence in the book.
        "(But he did not come.)(And the Boys dieing up there,)

(106)

--------Greenleaf says to me "I have a beef's liver in my haversaek lets go and cook it and have some thing to eat", By this time we were out of rations almost entirely, having coffee, and a hard tack or so left, So we slipped off down through the weeds, seeing the glimmer of a camp fire we walked in that direction, Here was a bed of coals and a frying pan half full of grease, just then a man thrust his head out of a tent near by and wanted to know what we were after, We told him we had a beef liver and wanted to fry some of it, "He says all right boys there is some hard bread in that barrel, help yourselves" This suited us exactly, we fryed liver ate hard bread, made coffee, as each man while on the march carried a tin can with a wire baillto it, and could hang it over a fire or held it on a stick, soon boil coffee, Completing our mid night meal we concluded we had work enough , Finding a lot of cotton we wrapped in our blankets for sleep, (It happened to be drivers of the Division train that we obtained our supplies of, Not forgetting to fill our haversacks with hard tack,(thanks)(this had to do us many days) ,

May 18th, Leave in an hour. The bridge is nearly finished, Black river is a deep muddy stream with steep banks, diffueult to cross, No firing as yet this morning, Reported Sherman is across with his Corps,(The 15th) Rebels on the retreat, At noon we marched over the bridge. As the artillery came across the water raised a few inches over the boards, All got safely across Black river and on the road to Vicksburg, Marched all afternoon through the dust,

up hill and down, rough country, Went into Bivouac some two miles from the rifle pits of Vicksburg,

May 19th.   Morning hot and dry. Advanced about 10 A M. Formed our first line
on the edge of a field with a tangled mass of bushes and vines in
front. Occasionally a musket bullet coming through the timber passed
over our heads singing its unfriendly song. Skirmishing. And some
Artillery firing. Regt's and Batteries moving forward to get in
position. Forward by flank and again in line so we keep moving.
Afternoon. In the many changes we came into a peach orchard to the
right of a large white house. Here the Officers cautioned every one
to be silent and quiet as we were right under the guns of Fort Hill.
We had climed up steep sides on deep ravines through brush, vines
and trees.The open fields are cultivated. Leaving the shelter of
the orchard the Regt flanked across an open corn field,(corn nearly
knee high).Seeing a new rubber blanket lying just out side of the
ranks I hesitated to step out and get it,unwilling to loose my place
in ranks. At the same instant a cannon shot from Ft Hill struck just
above us passing over our heads and under the feet of four men in
                                                   but higher up on the slope of the hill.
another Regt' also marching parallel with us. Knocking down the whole
four. They arose from a cloud of dust and all escaped unhurt, jumping
up laughing and moved on with their Regt'.Glanceing over my shoulder I
could see in an angle of the rebel Fort . (Fort Hill on the Jackson r
road), the cannoneers working a small gun while we were in full view
and not more than three or four hundred yards distant. They fired shot
after shot while we kept up a lively dodgeing and soon reached cover,
I let the rubber blanket go-
The 95th Ills charged and were repulsed with loss. We could hear the
boys cheer but could not see them.Under fire more or less nearly all
day only a few men wounded in our Regt

May 20th. Skirmishing all around. Sherman is close up on the right.
          Our lines are open to the Yazoo River, Bread is coming that way.
          5 P M. The rebels can not work a single gun on the out side works
          On account of our sharpshooters and skirmishers hidden in the
          brush , behind logs, along the edges of ravines. 6 P M. Nothing
          to eat all day , Boys firéing away. No artillery firing,
          Bivouac in the shelter of the hills, out of reach of the rebel fire,

May21st,   Firing quite lively this morning, Planted several batteries
during the past   night.Sharp shooters keep the rebels from
working their guns, Company "B on picket. Our men and the rebs
talking back and forth along the lines all night, Seems strange
to talk this way apparently friendly and then shoot at each other,

May 22d,   We have found a sheltered position in a ravine where we bivouac,
Cool and fine this morning, Batteries being planted, Rifle pits
dug as near as posible. Getting ready for an assault upon the
enemys works, To charge at 2 P M, Formed our ranks marched out
through the ravines and hollows. Finally took position on the
slope of a hill barely cover from the rebel fire, We formed in
column of Companies right in front closed en mass, As it happened
our Co was at the foot of the hill.The intention was to forward
and deploy into line on the brow of the hill then advance ,
Lying here waiting for other Regt's to get in position and fob
the word to forward, Brush and timber cut and slashed in the
valleys while the hill tops could be swept bare by the rebel fire,
While here chewing canes that were growing at our feet, to keep
our minds from what we knew was coming,a wood pecker lit on an
old dead snag sounding a tattoo with his bill then flew away
with a "churp¶(Happy woodpecker,)   Saw a man in our uniform
unarmed,only a haversack over his shoulder, Started to walk up
the hill to the right of the column lying there,He reached
nearly the top when a musket bullet struck him in the shoulder
and sent him whirling, He came on down the hill and landed on a
brush pile "kerslap" there he sat looking so foolish, I had to
laugh in spite of the deadly surroundings,I never knew who he
was or what became of him or what he was trying to do there,
After a long wait the word came to "Forward, Every man raised to
his feet and all moved forward the front Companies advanced to
the crest of the hill and were fairly swept off their feet by the
most deadly, concentrated,cross and enfilading fire,we were ever
under spread death and destruction in our ranks, sceing the
ground ahead was covered with slashed trees and brush that no
man could get through on a charge, besides a ravine to cross
before climing the opposite slope crowned by the rebel----

--breast works, and this ravine and all entervending space was slashed
full of brush and tree tops cut and lopped in every direction, almost
utterly impossible for a man to crawl through, No line could be
maintained under such conditions,It was over 100 yards from the brow
of the hill behind whose slope we lay,to the reb"entrenchments, Their
rifle pits and breast works well constructed not a man visible unless
he rashly showed him-self in his eagerness to fire at the advancing
" Yankees"The whole Regt' wilted and immediatly fell back under cover,
After loosing quite a number of men, Col Nevius fell at the head of
the Regt' leading them on, A musket ball struck him about the center
of the forehead from which the blood and brain was flowing,I saw the
boys carry his body down to the ravine out of the fire, A number of
the boys crawled off in the brush behind old logs and began sharp
shooting on their own hook, We now changed position and moved over to
the right,Our first formation would have been all right provided
the ground had been clear of obstructions, Some of us might have
reached the rebel intrenchments, but our losses would necessarily have
been very heavy, However our skirmishers did all they could to keep
them down while we were making efforts to charge , the Artillery also
contributed shot and shell over our heads and across to the rebs ,
Some captured amunition the shells burst shortly after leaving the
muzzle of the gun, at times not very pleasant for us, While near the
crest of the hill in this position we were exposed to an artillery
fire from Fort Hill. Here we lost 30 men in about five minutes.I
could see the gunners handling the one gun they could play on us,
In the mean time three flags were planted on the angle to the right,
Neither our men nor the enemy could get these flags, the 30th Ohio.
7th Mo men planted their Colors,and some of the 14th and 17th Wis
boys got in the ditches, Had to stay there until after dark before
they could crawl out, Late in the afternoon once more the word came
to forward, Knowing it would be useless, However we set our teeth
and determined to try, (Genl Ransom had appeared on the side hill
fully exposed th the fire and ordered Col Nevius to forward his Regt,
this was done as mentioned above),Forward we went , but such a tre--
mendous and withering fire met us that it seemed as if nothing human
could stand before it, Entirely disheartened we just seemed to flatten
out and as a Regt dropped back to the shelter of the ravine, _____

--Our cooks were back in the rear and boiled beef with out salt,
All we have in the ration line, I had tied a chunk of beef in a rag
and fastened this to my belt thinking, I would be hungry before we
returned to bivouac, about noon this had spoiled, Our artillery plumping
in shot and shell from every hill top, the sharp crack of rifles and
muskets. the drift of the wounded to the rear, fighting all around.
We now lay on a slope where we could not return the fire, but was safe
from their bullets, Darkness came on, the firing died away, Before I knew
it Tom Lewis and myself were sound asleep, Some time in the night I
was awakened by Tom pulling my shoulder "Saying they are moving out",
come along", We could see dark forms moving down the valley, We
followed but soon lost in the gloom found ourselves on a hill side.
Being fearful of getting too near the rebel works We lay down at the
foot of a large cotton wood tree and went to sleep again, Seemed like
we had hardly closed our eyes when Tom again awakened me, And there
we was in full view of the rebel rifle pits, the sun shining brightly.
We soon found our way down the ravine and a little further on came to
the Company.

May 23d,
Our position now is parallel to the rebel rifle pits, In a deep hell
hollow sheltered from their fire, We leveled places on the side
hill. Put up some forks and poles covered with brush, This is our
Bivouac, Hot, Some fine springs of water but we have to run the guantlet
to get our canteens filled, Cannon and musketry, No reply from the
rebel batteries, They have not fired a dozen shots to day, Sharp--
shooters firing at our skirmishers, A box of hard tack" arrived, Boys
knocked it open with the butt of a musket, It was soon distributed,
Each one helping himself, After being without three days this was
highly appreciated, and soon disposed of. (Best tasting bread we
ever ate),

May 24th, Sunday, Hot and dry, Firing the same as usual. Now and then a
shot from the rebel cannon, Boys watching closely. Last night the
rebels put cotton bales on their Forts and rifle pits in front of our
Brigade, Major Coats came to day to take Command of the Regt'.
No more charging, It is useless to try to charge over these hills,
The ravines and hollows full of a tangled mass of limbs and brush a
man can hardly walk through let alone charging with a musket and
                                                                   -----

-----amunition, Their works are built to rake every hill with a cross fire.

6 P M. The boys have had a rest to day, artillery men and all but
skirmishers on duty, Rebels saucy as ever, However these attacks
proved to the "Troops of the Invincible Army of the Tennessee", That
their breasts were insufficient to surmount the difficulties in the
way,

Detailed for picket, As the lines advance each man carries a spade or
shovel.then halt and go to digging a hole and the quicker the better,

Threw the dirt in front until the hole is deep enough to protect the
digger,Then turn and dig to the right, By morning a rifle pit will be
excavated as long as the line, Lay down the spade and take the musket,
Because the supprised enemy will immediatly open fire. The lines move
forward and the digging is done in the night,A man with musket,40
rounds, a spade. one days rations and santeen full of water, in the
darkness moves up as far as possible then digs, In this way the lines
are advanced night after night,

May 25th,Early this morning finds us in the rifle pits, My position was at
an angle exposed off to the right, having a spade I soon fixed the
ditch deep enough to protect Me from right, left. and front,I stuck
a row of little canes that were growing near along the top in order
to hide my cap when looking over,Their line of works is about 200
yards in front, I aimed at the top of their pits and fired, I got a
return shot quickly. struck the dirt about two inches below the top'
deep enough so it did not go through, We exchanged a few shots but as
I had no protection for my head concluddedte rest a while,Not a man
could be seen on their works, The man next te my left was located
behind a stump that happened th be in that part of the line, He also
opened fire, got a shot in return that hit the stump making the
splinters fly, It was so close he turned pale and sat down,
We kept watch abd firing occasionally until 4 P M, Flag of truce was
set up along the works. Cease firing, This is to bury the dead that
were killed in the charges of the 19th and 22d, The bodies had lain
so long in the hot sun their faces turned black and fingers like
birds claws, All that could be done was to shovel dirt over them
as they lay. One or two were lying near the pits we were in,

----The rebels raised up all along the lines, stood, and sat on top of the
works. We did the same, Looking at each other, dressed in grey and
"butternut" uniforms there seemed to be a lot of them, we in our blue
just like 'gophers" poping up out of the ground in all directions,
More or less talking no firing, as it was to last until 8 30 P M,
Two rebel Colonel's Holland and Stever met in a ravine with our Lieut
(Vernay) Shook hands and chatted, together quite friendly, Our Lieut
taking some letters to mail for them, Col Stever was dressed in blue,
the other in grey, As the night came on all was deathly still. Not a
shot any where down the lines, No sound except the talking between
the pickets, Some of them exchanged tobacco and coffee,
About 10 P M, we were relieved and returned to camp, after being on
duty 24 hours, Cant' get in our rifle pits in day light so many places
not yet covered, Have to " turkey" in these places, That is double up
and run half bent, letting them shoot at us,

May 26th, The sun comes down hot this morning. There was no firing last night
Pickets agreed not to fire at each other, Quiet and still,
Finally "whang! went a musket(every body hunt your hole) followed
by a spattering of shots all down the lines, Soon the artillery
joined in and firing lively for a while then died down towards
noon, From 3 P M til sun down pretty brisk again, Charging is now
"played out" "Seige work begins.

May 27th, Hot, Every thing is quiet only a musket shot once in a while,
The rebel Joe Johnson is reported to be at Black river with 40 000
men, After cleaning my Enfield rifle I have loaded with eight revolver
balls, I calculate to give it a sling" and slay a whole Regt' our
rifles are sighted for 800 yards, kill a man that distance if we can
hit him,

May 28th Skirmishing, Digging rifle pits, Planting cannon,, Evening cool,
rec'd letters from home,

May 29th, Lively cannonade all along the lines, Genl Grant calculates he
can send 600 shells per minute into Vicksburg, The rebels are
firing short pieces of rail road iron at our batteries, We can
expect a train of cars next, 11 A M, light rain, 5 P M Heavy ---

--- Artillery firing on the right, left and center, No reply from the
    Rebels except a rail road Iron now and then,

May 30th, Morning sun rose clear and hot, Birds singing also the bullets,
    Skirmishing as usual, One of our Gun Boats sunk a day or so ago,
    They silenced 13 rebel guns, all but one big rifle they call
    "Whistling Dick", 6 P M, Heavy firing, X

May 31st, Sunday morning at about three o'clock we were awakened by the keen
    sharp report of a battery of four Parriot guns that had been
    planted during the night just above our camp' They were firing
    over our heads from the opposite side of the ravine,The keen rifle
    like reports fairly raised us out of our beds, As the shots
    passed they cut the leaves and small branches off the trees,
    Kept up a steady fire until day light, 8 A M firing died out.
        Reported seven men captured with 30 pounds gun caps apiece trying
        to get in to Vicksburg,
        We Bivouac
June 1st,   We are in a deep ravine just to the right of a large white house
    on the Jackson road with Fort Hill to our left and front,Genl
    Logan's Head Quarters back of the White house, No tents, Some
    of the boys have burrowed in the opposite side hill, making caves
    to sleep in, We like the brush shelter the best,Firing when ever
    any one exposes himself. Advancing pits and batteries, covered ways
    and approaches,each day and night,

June 2d' Heavy firing of musketry last night on the left, We since learned
    the rebels tryed to break out and were driven back, 7 P M, Cool
    not much firing, J D Lyons of our Co' built what he called a look
    out, None of the Boys would help him so he dragged up twelve poles
    Got some hogshead staves and plased these in double with the poles
    for frame and clay banked up on the out side until after much hard
    work he had a lookout sure enough,From this perch he had a fair view
    of the Rebel works. A board across the south west corner served for
    a seat with a loop hole in front to fire through. After spending
    about two weeks work, (The Boys in the mean time hooted at him for
    building such a thing),So one morning just before day light he got up
    in this concern took a seat and pushed his Enfield rifle through the
    port and sighted it, Just back of Fort Hill he saw two"Jonnies"_____

(113) B

May 30th, X

The Gun Boats engaged the water batteries.
Above the thunder of the cannon we could hear at intervals
a sharp heavy report,followed by the unusual scream of a
shell,(We learned later this was the big 6 inch rifle the
Rebs called "Whistling Dick" With it they sunk the "Cincinnati"
in the bend of the river,)
Now and then a rebel sharpshooter climbs a tree for a better
view of our approaches and to enable him to pick off some
of our men that happen to be exposed.We soon locate him ,then
cut loose and a few shots and he tumbles out of that.
We got these sharp shooters every time they climb up in trees.
Never takes very long to locate them, A puff of smoke tells
the tale. We never try that game on our side, but keep close to
the ground.

——sitting in the smoke of a small fire eating breakfast, He first sighted at one then the other, Finally decided to take the right hand man.
(only about 75 yards),Aiming,pulled the trigger, As he did soo some
one just west of him over their breastworks must have been watching
for at the report of his musket from the noise under and around on the
out side of that look out there must have been a dozen shots fired,
However three bullets penetrated and went through these hard seasoned
staves (two thickness) and one hitting the opposite side, He was'nt
long in getting down to the bottom of that elevated lookout. The break
break of day did not catch any of the Boys in thatoplace, But after
dark it was a fine place to watch the mortershells and the night
firing of artillery &c, To gaze at the stars and wonder whatr they
were doing at home .

June 3d. Morning cool and quiet only a stray shot now and then, Afternoon
cool with some rain, Three Divisions are coming to reenforce the
Army around Vicksburg, Men and wagons were sent out in the country
and gathered from the plantations a lot of shovel plows,(used in
cultivating corn and cotton), The Blacksmithsoflattened the steel
plows and cut a slot large enough for an Enfield rifle to pass through
and be sighted, These we set on top of our rifle pits and covered with
gunny sacks filled with sandy clay soil that abounds here,in these
bluffs. placed over the loop hole so as to shade on both sides,
In the morning they can see through our ports and in the evening we
can see through theirs,We stopped this by shading with these sacks
as well as forming a protection for our heads.Logs are also used
making the loop holes under, But a cannon shot will knock the logs
off,While watching when we see the holeodarkened we fire,Because we
knew some one is looking out, They do the same.Both sides get sharp
enough to remedy this by shading so the light will not shine through

(A by word, "Have your shoes blacked and be ready to charge at
   2 o'clock,)
(The man who was censured by his Capt' for having a rusty musket,
   remarked"He had the brightest shovel over in the trenches of any
   man on the job),"

June 4th, Aroused out of sleep this morning at 3 30 and formed line of
battle, Expecting the Rebels to give us a call, But they did
not come,The muskets and cannon keep talking to the rebels the same
as usual, Very hot dry and dusty, The rebs opened a battery of six
guns on our left, The Boys put a stop to that in less than an hour,
They can not work a single gun on this side of Vicksburg, Some times they
load up in the night and fire a morning salute at us, close the ports and
quit during the day.On a detail to go out back of the lines in the woods
and pull down grape vines from the trees, wild vines, they bear a grape
called muscadines, These vines were brought in and used to make gabions &
for embrasures, A circle of stakes is driven into the ground and the
grape vines were withed and twisted around the stakes, These basket like
cylinders are set up on each side of the embrasures,Then filled with
clay and soil to keep the bank up on either side,8p the cannon can be
fired,At the same time protect the cannoneers, After firing the
embrasures are stopped with bags of cotton to keep the sharpshooters
from picking off the artillerymen.

June 5th, Morning hot, Firing about the same, One of Co'sK's boys just
killed in the rifle pits, shot through the head.
Detailed to go to the Yazoo Landing after forage, Dusty and hot
marching along with the wagons,in the dust , so many pass this way to
the Landing after rations and ammnition,Takes hard tack for the Boys
and powder for the guns,Reached the landing, A good many boats here,
Loaded up and on the return, Can hear the boom of cannon, Musketry
sounds like fire crackers at this distance, So many men get killed
and wounded while prowling around in places they ought not to be,
Every open space is watched by rebel sharpshooters, They generally hit
every one so exposed,Going after water with a lot of canteens on his
back, A bullet from the "rebs" cut a hole through several so they would
not hold water, This at one of the open places they had to pass,

June6th, Cool this morning. Not much firing. There is an old log above
our bivouac on the crest of the hill, Roberts and I go up there
after dark and sit on this log,,Watching the shells, -------

--- The mortar flats are three miles below on the river, We see a flash like

like distant lightning way off down the river south west from where we

are sitting, Then a spark, Just a round spot of fire mounting up higher an

and higherSeems to go by jumps, this is the shell as it turns over and

over in the air, As it reaches the highest point and just as it turns to

descend we hear the report of the mortar, Booming and echoing over the

hills and on down the river, Following the flight of the shell,(if it

bursts in the air)we see a blood red flash of fire, Then the sound of the

shell whistling and trembling on the air until it reaches the place of

explosion,Then comes the echoing report with a terrific roar, These

thirteen inch shells if they happen to reach a building of any kind in

their flight and burst are apt to tear things pretty badly, Many of them

burst in the ground with a muffled roar, These are sent in only at night.

The grandest fire works nightly.

June 7th, Sunday, Had to get up at three o'clock this morning to help plant
a battery of four guns on the hill above our camp,about 400 yards
from the enemys works, Hot, hotter than any day yet,
4 P M Preaching.

June 8th, Hot as usual, not much firing , It does not seem possible that
20000 rebels are as close to us as they are, We talk with them
from the rifle pits nearly every night back and forth, joking,
and some times "cussing", Asking about grub &c, Trade canteens,
Ours are of tin covered with blanket wool,keeps the water cool
longer, while theirs are made of red cedar,

June 9th, Every thing about as usual, The "rebs" no nearer surrender than evr
ever, very hot and the dust from one to four inches deep, Not
much cannonading but the sharp shooters keep up a pretty hot
fire, Not many killed on either side, We were aroused about 10
o'clock just after a thunder storm and heavy rain by crys of "fall
in", "a spade" "a shovel quick",Tom Edland and myself bunked
together, We raised up to see what was the matter, While Tom
Lewis dressed buckeled on his cat'ridge box grabbed his musket,
ready for any event in the fighting line(Tom's always ready",)
Quite an uproar on the opposite side of the ravine, by this
time some lit candles, It seems that three of the boys were---

---sleeping in one of those hill side caves,The heavy rain caved in

the roof and buried or partly so the three,They with the spades soon dug
and dragged them but, all mud and wet, Quite a crowed had gathered, It was
soon over. And as the boys passed on to their quarters one little Dutchman
'n a peculiar whineing voice, Said " T'was a mity qoot ting' that wan of
em' had 'is 'ed out so's he could holler".Edland just rolled and laughed.
So did the rest of us, Quiet soon reigned as well as the weather, by this
time it was midnight,dark and thick with mist and rain,

WE generally undressed, some times leaving on our pants in order to rest
well unless we expected to be called during the night,

June 10th,   Very wet after the rain last night, At work from 6A M until 11
            A M "Throwing up breast werkk for cannon within 2oo yaþds of
            the Rebel rifle pits,fair range, I" would dig up a shovel full
            of the yellow clay threw it up in front then jump up and wave the
            shovel at the rebs, then "juke! How the bullets would sing over
our head   while we were down behind the bank,
            McAlisters four gun battery on the point of hill above our
            quarters are c 24 pounders. we would take empty peach cans that
            just fit these guns, fill them with bullets, pieces of iron, taps
            or bolts. and carry these up to the artillery men to fire over
            to the rebels, The cans would be torn to pieses and scatter
            the contents far and wide,Raining most of the time up to 3 P M.
            Stopped raining sun shining, Peek and I are studying short hand,
            I have Pitmans manuel. Having piece of paper and pencil can
            work at it any time while off duty,

June 11th, There was heavy firing on the left last night, Cloudy but cool,
            Genl Logan has in position a nine inch gun brought aroundd from
            the Gun Boats (A Dalgren)fired several-shots, There is a 1o inch
            gun to be put in position soon as possible, Heavy details to
            plant more guns, We are closing around the"rebels" fast, Logan's
            big gun kept up a lively firing nearly all day, Tore one side of
            Ft Hill nearly down. After each discharge a hole would be torn
            out large enough apparantly to drive a team and wagon through,
            One of the largest and best Forts they have on our front command-
            ing the Jackson road. 8 P M all quiet, no fireing,

June 12th. Pleasant and clear but not so warm as before the rain. Fireing co
                                                                    ------

continues the same as usual. While it is so hot the artillery men
rest in the shade at noon time, The rebels fired four shells at
our big gun, The shells burst in air and did not hurt any one,
The Chippewa Indians of the 14th Wis Inftry, make good skirmishers
One we call "John" is a fine sharp shooter, Goes out by himself,
Crawls until he finds a secure place, Then lay and watch, When he
sees an opportunity to hit , after careful aim he fires then rolls
over and over to get away from the return bullets that are sure to
come, The smoke reveals his hiding place.Late in the day he generally
comes in grinning as he goes by our bivouac, passes on up to Ransom's
Head Quarters for a "jigger". He knows its there for him,
These Indians make good skirmishers and sharp shooters, They dont
like to fight in line, Do best on their own hook.

June 13th,Hot as usual, Pretty sharp firing this morning No reply from the
enemy's cannon. At dark they sent over two or three shells but
did no harm, They must have a mortar back under the hill so
placed our artillery can't reach them.Some of the boys wounded
while on fatigue duty,

June 14th, Sunday. Warm and pleasant, Lively musket firing, One of the
14th Wis boys shot through the neck and jaw, is alive and will
probably live, A Corpl while sighting his gun was killed by a
rebel sharp shooter, shot through the top of the head, He
belonged to one of the 2d Ills Batteries, The enemy sent over
shells pretty lively all day, from their concealed mortars, After
every shell our artillery would concentrate their fire and fairly
tear the hill into fragments where they supposed the mortars
be located., none of our shots could reach them under the hill. They
shelled out the 31st Ills so they had to move quarters,they were
just to the left of our bivouac, We had to dodge pretty lively all
afternoon, kept us watching especially when the shells burst over
our heads and the pieces go humming in all directions, They must be
9 inch shell, For some of the peices will weigh 15 to 30 pounds,
They came pretty close but none of our boys were hit by them,
We hear the report of the mortar, but the shell comes sneaking
and bursts before we are aware of it, leaving a round white cloud of
smoke to drift away, on the summer air.

June 15th

Morning cool. Lively cannonade, Companies "A B" C and"D detailed for picket. Co "C was on the right, "A and "B on the left and Co"D in the center,with some of the 14th Wis boys, One of their men was wounded in the arm and neck slightly. Two or three of Co "D,s men wounded. Sergt Edland with six privates, myself among the number on the reserve A fatigue party working on the hill planting a battery,(At this time of year some people plant corn.) The rebels kept up a hot fire of musketry nearly all night none of the fatigue party hit, being protected by the breast work in front. Our advanced rifle pits and batteries in our front are only about 200 yards from the enemys lines, Some of the pits are much nearer,

June 16th Appearance of rain, Heavy firing, An advanced Fort which we call "Fort Ransom, (Genl Ransom) (ᴧ planed it), Is about 200 yards from Ft Hill. Had to dig a road wide enough for the gun carriage to pass, this road is covered with timbers laid across and dirt piled on top thus making a covered way,sufficient to protect us from bullets and shell, Then we have connecting trenches, rifle pits and covered ways to enable us to pass from our quarters clean up to the most advanced pits without being exposed to the enemys fire, One or two uncovered places that we have to dodge or make a run for it,Taking our chances of being hit by the"minnie" bullets, These are the places where the fellows that are "poking around"get hit, The ground is honey combed with trenches, One has to be posted to travel here,

June 17th, Morning fair, The rebels fired volleys all last night at our working parties,Part of the morning and most of the afternoon the shells came over every 15 minutes, Many burst over our heads,No damage, What must it be in the City where our bullets and shell are hissing day and night,? Heavy cannonade from our guns all day,

June 18th, Cloudy and cool, Rather quiet, Not much firing, Not as much as usual. Been lying around all day about half sick. Company went on picket, Did not go with them, Corpl A Drake and Private J Spire, Promoted to Sergt's. Privates, T N Lewis, C Warbus, L Coleman, and Geo D Carrington, Promoted to the elevated rank of Corporals, To take rank from May 1st, 1863, May they never disgrace their stripes,

(120)

June19th, Cool and very pleasant for June in this part of the world, Boys e

came in all right this morning, No one hurt, Lively firing from our

artillery, died out at noon, Not well, but not on the sick list,

June 20th, Day light found us in line, As we supposed for a charge, or to

support some movement, But were dismissed for dinner :with the

order to be ready to fall in at a moments notice, Logans men are dig--

ging into the rebel Ft Hill, 4 P M, They are shooting at the rebs
from their own parapet,

June 21st, Cool with fine breeze, On the sick list, 17 men reported sick
this morning in Co "B, Not much firing, One of the 14th Wis. boys
killed in the pits,

June 22d, Very warm and dry, Heavy firing, muskets and cannon, 1o A M quiete

not much firing, The cannoneers as it is getting so warm fire
early in the morning, lay in the shade at noon then open fire again
in the evening, and some times during the night a few rounds to keep
them agitated in the City, A regular serving on one of the 9 inch
guns had completed ten years of service in the Army, His time was out,
"said he would stand guard to night in regular turn for the last
time",About midnight while walking back and forth in rear of the
gun a musket bullet passed through his head killing him instantly,
we all thought it pretty hard after being in the service so long
to be killed the last night, Such is the fate of war,

June 23d, Warm as usual, One of the 11th men wounded while on duty in the
rifle pits, to day, The 14th Wis are being paid off two months
pay,2 P M Not a great deal of firing, But a good deal of
digging going on around here, The rebels hold out well, But we feel
sure of them any how and before many days we expect to march into
Vicksburg, God grant we may with out any more blood shed,
4 P M, Paid two months pay $ 26 oo, Dark, Some rain, Heavy musket
firing on the left, 8 P M, Orders to be ready to fall in at a moments
notice, Fighting on the left off towards the river, Heavy firing,

(121)

June 24th. Morning finds matters the same as usual. We were not called,
Men on the left drove the rebs back with some loss, 1 P M,
Firing as usual, Reported Port Hudson taken,

June 25th.   Hot as usual, Heavy fireing all around, Our lines are about
13 miles long, Reported Joe Johnson is on the retreat and
Sherman's men after him, 9 A M. Orders to fall in to support
Logan.s men who are going to charge on the rebel Ft Hill, at
about 2 o'clock, They had undermined and placed a large amount
of powder, This was exploded throwing up a column of dirt, dust,
and smoke . Not much of a report, But just a spout of dust high
in the air, A blubber you might call it mixed with timbers,
boards and men, The 45th Ills, armed with short Enfield rifles
and sabre bayonets rushed into this crater driving back the enemy
Or at least taking posession of the crater, Supported by the 20th
Ills, and the 124th, Ills , the 11th in reserve, The Lieut Col and
Major of the 45th were both killed being the first men on the
parapet, Heavy and close musketry with the artillery was poured
in to keep the rebs back until a foot hold could be secured,
As there was only a bank of earth pretty badly shattered at that
between the combatants, The 45th boys lost a good many of their
bayonets by throwing them over at the enemy, the fight was close
and desperate, Night finds the boys in posession of half of
the Fort, The rebs the inside half, Our loss is not very heavy,
But suppose they must have lost a good many as our cannon had a
cross fire in the rear of the Fort they were much exposed in
going in or out, Two twelve pound Howitzers in Ft Ransom rendered
good service, The sharp shooters and the 14th Wis kept up quite
a lively fire all night,
Our artillery is becoming very accurate in their fire, I notice
Mc Allisters gunners can burst a shell in a sack of sand on top
   the Rebel works nearly every time, In using sperical case,
Which is a round shell with a dial of lead marked from one to
ten, for range of one mile they cut the dial at 5 that is 5
seconds to the mile, the shell bursts one mile from the muzzle of
the gun,

(122)

June 26th, Morning finds us the same as last night,"Ready". Logans men
firing to keep the rebs down while they are digging and preparing
a cover to protect themselves,also make room for more men.They are p
planting two guns,
2 P M. The same as yesterday. Orders to be ready to fall in at a
moments notice, 4 P M, Logans men have fallen back, having lost about
250 men and gained nothing. The rebels threw over hand grenades,####
Where these failed to explode our boys tossed them back to their
friends, they also used 6 pound shells, lighting the fuse and roll
them down among our boys,many of these were hurled back and exploded
on the other side, several were wounded by these shells,It was
desperate fighting with only a wall of earth between, Six Companies
of the 11th detailed for picket, "B was posted in a deep ravine,
The others in the rifle pits and Fort Ransom to support the working
party,

June 27th, Warm and dry, Lively firing this morning, Relieved from picket
at day light,Later on going up the covered way I met two men carrying
Capt Kenyon of Co "K, on a stretcher, He had been in Ft Ransom, In
taking a peep out of one of the embrasures a rebel sharp shooter
caught sight of his face and fired,.the bullet plowing a furrow across
the right temple.He had one hand supporting his head while the blood
was trickling between his fingers, A close call,

June 28th, Hot this morning, We are around Vicksburg like a picket fence,
It is "Hello Yank: And how are you Jonnie", Jonnie Rebs", While
talking last night some one asked "How do you like your new General,
"What General? "Why Gen'l Starvation", Then they all laughed,"Hello
Yank!" Well what is it ? "When you'ns coming in", "Soon's we get hungry
for mule beef", ha ha, We hear they are down to mule beef now, short
rations, Our men got hold of some blue beans,"Refugee beans," they call
them, they are fine eating however, One of the Boys was sitting while
eating his dinner with a plate of these beans on his knees, A minnie bullet
struck the under side of a limb over head--

###

Hand grenades,

An elongated cast iron shell about as large as a goose
egg,with a precussion cap in the front end, In the rear
end a stick fitted with paper some thing like the feathers
on an arrow,This is to balance and make the grenade go
straight to the mark, the end strikes and explodes the cap,
also bursts the shell,

The six pound shell is fitted with a fuse and cut long enough
to throw over the works, Where the fuse was burning and
sufficiently safe it was grabbed up and thrown back, bursting
on their side, however the Boys take chances when they pick
them up,of having the explosion while in their hands,
this seldom if ever occured,If the shell did not burst on our
side they generally got the full benefit om theirs,

---turned downward and passed through his leg making four holes,
This in a deep ravine where it seemed almost impossible for a bullet
to reach any one in passing over, When Logan blowed up the Rebel Fort
some five or six white men and two or three darkeys went up in the
dust and dirt. One negro fell inside our lines with a broken leg,
"Said,"When he was going up , "Met his master coming down",

June 29th, Very warm, Co "B on fatigue,-Worked from 11 A M,,until 1 P M,
The boys in the pits kept the rebs down while we were digging
and cutting brush, preparding ways and roads, So we could make
a quick rush over their works, Powers and myself worked right
under the rebel embankment to clear the ground so at a few jumps
we could get in the rebs' works, My!but it is hot the sun beats
down like fire,Boys on the look out keeping them down as they
can not fire on us unless exposed themselves,We can throw a
chip over where they are in their trenches,They have no shells
handy or they would be rolling them down for ourbenefit, They
know as well as we do that we are going to celebrate the fourth,
we are also protected by our entrenchments on either flank.
At 1 P M, We crawled out and passed through the trenches and
covered ways back to quarters, Have now 2oo cannon in position
15o rounds served to each gun will make things lively around
here on the 4th!,

June 3oth, Hot,Mustered for pay at 9 A M,Firing continues all around, We
                                     and trenches,
are now close up with rifle pits,,Cannon on every hill top,

July 1st, Co" B" detailed for twenty four hours in the pits, About 5o yards
from the enemys works, Our trenches are deep enough so we can
stand up and lean against the front bank while firding through
the port, Then we have seats cut on the back side so we can sit
down to rest, also have a shade fixed up to keep the hot sun
off our heads,As it is very hot in these trenches, A little
shelf dug in front to place our cat'ridges in order to have them
handy, We fire 2oo rounds per day that constitutes a days work
while in the pits, In our front is a large oak tree just inside
their trenches we aim to skip the bullet over their works and---

----and hit this troc, It is pretty well splintered, From the English
Enfield rifle minnie bullet(58 calabre) This bullet is an inch long
with a wooden plug in the end, As the powder explodes this plug is
driven in and expands the lead causing it to fit in the rifles,
Giving it the whirling motion and holds it steady in its flight,
The rebels use the same, Their grey uniforms and Enfield rifles
furnished by England, "Two eoutomers are better than one",
We are now expert marksman and so are the rebs", Yet we fire all day
just at the top of their works with out seeing a single man,
Any part of a man exposed is plugged immediatly, The main object is
to keep bullets singing, shells bursting, and solid shot whistling
over their works to keep them down and draw their fire so they will
expend their amunition, With supplies cut off , short of rations
and amunition they must soon give up, 12 noon. Cain of Co "C killed.
I often put in two bullets and fire them, notice two little puffs of
dust as they hit the top of the enemys works, When the musket is foul
we load, then pour in water enough to fill the barrel, (from the
canteen), then fire, this cleans and cools, When the barrel gets too
hot from rapid fireing we sit down and rest, read the papers if we
happen to have one, (Having seats prepared in the clay wall.)
As night comes on the firing does away, and the talking begins,
Some times we agree not to shoot while the pickets who are often
only a few yards apart posted between the lines, trade tobacco, and
canteens, Their cedar for our tin,

July 2d, Relieved at 8 A M, by a detachment from the 72d Ills, and returned
to camp, Corpl Charles Hindman, of Co I was asked,, (Last night), "What
time is it", He struck a match looked at his watch and replyed
"One o'clock", He then turned , looked out at a loop hole and
was immediatly killed by a bullet that entered, just below the
left eye, The boys brought him out and back to camp, He was a
fine young fellow, we all thought a great deal of him, It was
pitch dark and how they managed to make such a hit as that we could
not understand, Companies "I and "B are both from Marshall County
Illinois,

July 3d, Heavy firing on the left last night. Lively cannonade this
morning. 10 A M, A flag of truce, They are going to surrender,
Hooraf!' Firding ceased. Heads pop up all along the lines on
both sides, Some one fired a musket, 'Down every body,' 'Hunt your
holes! No more firing and gradually the heads come up again,
Sitting on top of the trenches looking at each other, thousands
of men,. At 4 P M. Genl Grant and Genl Pemberton met near an oak
tree that grew in an open space on the outer slope of Ft Hill.
To agree on terms of surrender.(Pemberton Oak the Boys call it),
Pemberton, wants it on conditions,
Grant, Says unconditional,
Pemberton, Well I'll go back and fight it out,
Grant, All right,use your own pleasure,
Pemberton, Leaves it to two of his Genl's,
Grant, To McPherson and Smith,
Night, No firding, Still as death, Terms of surrender not agreed
upon. Boys in good spirits, 8 P M, Mail came in, r c'd letter
from Father, (We are going to be fooled on celebrating the 4th
with musket and cannon if we dont look out,)

July 4th,
So quiet last night could hardly sleep, No firding this morning.
The white flag flies on the rebel works. 10 A M, Pemberton has
surrendered, Prisoners to be patroled, About 30 ooo.1loo ~~pieces~~ men
of artillery light and heavy, Heavy guns in the water batteries,
Light artillery around the entrenchments, Large amount of small
arms. Equipments &c &c,   The Rebels were starved out having
lived on mule beef for the past four days and perhaps longer.
The Rebel Regt's marched out at 1o o'clock and stacked arms
out side their works, hung cat'ridge boxes on the stacks,
Laid up the flags mostly a cross on a brown field, I saw no
regular colors, The "Bonnie Blue Flag" must have been hidden or
carried away by its friends, As it did 'nt show up,
Silently they marched out and silently they marched back, We stod -
looking on Genl Logans Division, Ransom's Brigade(being attached to Logans
Division during the seige),Formed to march in. Lieut Dean
placed me at the left of the first platoon, However we marched
in column of fours our usual formation, As we passed down the
Jackson road_____

(126)

---through the dust and heatthe rebels sat on each side looking on,
They were taking it easy now while we had to march in the dust and
take posession, We marched down to the Court House and at 2 15 P M,
Stacked arms, The Stars and stripes: were soon flying from the dome
of the Court House, We had now an opportunity to look around,
I saw mule meat on the block in the rebel commissary, Its true they
ate it no other meat to be had, we cut off supplies sure enough,
It seems they had rice and beans with 4 ounces of flour per day
to the man,. After chatting with the Rebs, occasionally handing out
a hard tack as some of them looked hungry,We fell in and marched out
to the North east angle of their works stacked arms, cooked some
"grub", I had a can of cove oysters in my haversack, with hard tack
I made a meal,(And so we celebrated our 4th of July.)

At 8 P M,Our Company is on guard duty,A road passes out side the work
near here, During the night many of the rebs were passed out,Saying
they was going home some to remain and others said they would fight
us again,They go afoot and carry blankets and rations, No arms,
Glad to get a chance to go, Some lived in Tennessee and others in
Mississipi, It is.nt likely they will be in the rebel Army very soon,
July 5th.   8 A M, And not relieved yet. From the looks of trees and the
rebel intrenchments they stood a terrible fire from our Batteries
andsmall arms, Their loss was about 150 per day killed and wounded,
A fire was kindled to cook rations and make coffee near by was
three limber chests of amunition for artillery, These chests were
planted in the ground to be safe from our fire during the seige,
Some of the Boys accasionally carried some of this powder and
exploded it in the fire, They scattered some on the ground for about
2 P M, These three chests blew up tearing the chests all to pieces,
as the cloud of white smoke went up it carried with it the leaves
from a large cotton wood tree standing near,several shells burst
high in the air, I was sitting near eating a cracker, As the powder
flashed I immediately pitched head first down the hill with a piece
of board about four feet long thrashing the ground after me, I reached
the cover of a brush pile and took refuge under it until the scare
was over,(finished my cracker,) Three men slightly wounded.
At 8 P M we were relieved from guard duty.

(127)

July 6th, Warm this morning, We find that the works here consist of one
line of rifle pits,with strong bastions and redoubts for cannon,
That they could not use for our watchful sharpshooters, In
making the loop holes for musket fire they used stripes of
boards about four inches wide, These were laid edge wise at an
angle so the outer ends were three or four feet apart, while
the inside ends were about two inches,   This enabled
                                      Thus,
them to get quite a range, Of course the top was covered to
protect the head, We can stand here now and look over the ground
between the lines that we fought and dug over so long, (47 days)
Two or three Divisons gone to Black river, Reported fighting
with Johnson's command. Logans Division stays in Vicksburg,
Prisoners coming in from the Big Black, Major Mc Kee is paroling
the prisoners as fast as possible, (The silver arrow is the badge
                                         of the 17th Corps),
(Genl Mc Phersons Order to the 17th Qorps,)

(127)B
"" Hotel De Vicksburg",

Bill of fare for July 1863,

"Soup --Mule tail,
Boiled--Mule bacon, with poke greens, Mule ham canvassed,

Roast-- Mule sirloin, Mule rump stuffed with rice, Saddle of mule a la arête,

Vegetables-- Boiled rice, rice hard boiled, hard rice any way,

Entrees-- Mule head stuffed a la Reb. Mule beef, jerked a la Yankee.
          Mule ears fricaseed a la gotch. Mule side, stewed, new style,
          hair on. Mule liver, hashed, a la explosion.

Side Dishes-- Mule salad, mule hoof soused, Mule brains, a la omelette.

                Mule kidneys, brains on ramrod.
                Mule tripe on half (parriot) shell.
                Mule tongue, cold a la bray,

Jellies-- Mule foot, Mule bone, a la trench.

Pastry --- Rice pudding. Poke berry sauce, Cottonwood berry pie,a la ironclad

           China berry tart,

Dessert--- White oak acorns. Beech nuts, Blackberry leaf tea. Genuine
           Confederate coffee,

Liquors-- Mississippi water, (Vintage 1692),very superior. $3,Limestone
          water, late importation! very fine;$3,75 spring water, Vicksburg,
          bottled up $4, extra,

          Meals at few hours, Gentleman to wait upon themselves, Any inatten-
          tion in service should be promptly reported at office, Jeff Davis
          &Co Props.

Card---   The proprietors of the justly celebrated Hotel de Vicksburg, having
          enlarged and refitted the same are now prepared to accommodate
          all who may favor them with a call. Parties arriving by the
          river ,or by Grants inland route will find Grape Cannister & Co's
          carriages at the landing; or any depot on the line of entrenchment
          Back Ball & Co. take charge of all baggage,

          No effort will be spared to make the visit of all as interesting
          as possible.

        " Note-- Amid all the horrible vicissitudes of grim war, strange
               humors within the leaguered wall of seamed,starving,desperate
               Vicksburg, would crop out and rebel humor rose above nature,
          When Vicksburg fell, a curious proof of this was found,
          A manuscript bill of fare, surmounted by a rough sketch of a
          mules head, crossed by a human hand holding a bowie knife. "

          * The menu reads as above and was captured by the Yanks on
            July 4th 1863."

July 7th, Rain last night,morning cooler. Doing guard duty near Fort Hill.
Visited the White House (as we call it) It stands on the Jackson
road opposite Ft Hill. The inmates left at the begining of the seige,
Probably went on to the City.No time to take any furniture with
them, As the Officers used it occasionally as a point of observation.
It was peppered by the rebels. I went in rooms where musket bullets
had gone clear through, Pictures hanging on the walls were torn by
bullets, paper and plaster hanging in shreds,To see a room with
carpet on floor. pictures on walls, furniture, chairs, tables, and
such, Then to look at the bullet holes,Is war indeed,

July 8th,
Our tents and mess chests came up and we established camp once
more on the hills north east of town, We have been with out
since April 26th the day we left camp at Millikins Bend.
This closes the Vicksburg Campaign,Of hard marches,Dust,heat.
Twenty days on five days rations,Three days without bread,
Battles, Skirmishes, The Seige of 47 days and fianl Victory,

July 9th , Quiet and cool , On guard, 35 rebels passed out during the night
all had their paroles, Going home,on their own account,wanted
to get away from the main column,

July 10th, Relieved from guard, Quietly in camp, The deathly stillness is
hard to bear,after so much heavy firing of cannon and musketry,

July 11th Hot morning, The Prisoners marched out with their paroles,
Several thousand, Some of them have had enough of war, all the
"rights" they want, and will go home the first chance,

July 12th, Cooler this morning, Reported Lee defeated in Pennsylvania,

July 13th, Hot on these hills, Went down town and returned sick,
Coming up to camp so hot seemed like I could hardly make it.
We sit in these tents and wipe the sweat off our faces all day,
nights cool, some mosquitos,

July 14th, Down sick with fever,

July 15th, The Regimental Doctor left a lot of powders, The boys help me
to take them and care for me, I lay in the tent with a red hot
fever,

July 17th, The last few days are almost a blank, I remember of staggering
down to the Capt's tent and signing the pay rolls, so sick
could hardly make it,

July 18th, The Regt left for Natchez, The sick men left behind to take
care of themselves and the Camp,

July 20th, Fever about gone, those powders are so large would break up
any thing, unless it is the Rebellion,

July 23d Cool and quiet this morning, Nearly well once more,
Ihave a dread of going to the Hospital so remained in my tent,
with the boys to help me I got along very well, they were very
kind, brought water from the spring which was very refreshing,

July 24th, Very warm, As fast as the men get well they leave to join the
Company at Natchez, Only two or three left to care for tents
and camp equipage, I drew rations for ten men so there is plenty
for the ones that remain,
Several hundred prisoners came in from Black River,

July 25th, Two Divisions came in from Black River,Quiet and hot in camp,
Days are fearful in the tents, nights cool. mosquitos thick.
Boys flash a lot of captured cannon powder in front of the tent
The smoke settles down and drives the "Skeeters" away,

July,26th, No news from the Regt. Boats with troops going up the river,

July 27th, Thunder storm last night, Wind blew the tents down, We have the
wedge tent now four men to each tent,Genjerally takes a man to
each pole to hold the tent down during these thunder gusts,
One on each side holding the edge of the canvas down to keep
the wind from getting under, We drive short forks in the ground
and lay poles or canes on and make a bunk on each side, Passage
in the middle between bunks,These are about a foot or so off
the ground, much better than sleeping on the bare ground,
Cool with showers,

(130)

July 28th,,   The third Brigade passed going out side to camp,

July 29th,   Quietly in camp, keeping pretty close to my tent,dont feel
              able to walk very much.

July 30th,   Received a letter from boys at Natchez, All in good spirits,
              Having gay times, Plenty of fruit and sweet potatos. The Regt
              is expected back, Cool and fine this morning,

July 31st, Days are all alike,

Aug 1st, Rain, cool and showery, No Regt yet, There is quite a number of
         colored people in the "Contraband Camps",some sickness,

Aug 2d, Warm. Three men of each Company to be furloughed for thirty days,
        Ten of us in quarters here, Regt at Natchez, Expect them every
        day,

Aug3d,   Moved camp about a mile nearer town, Hot, Quite a job for ten men
          convalesents to handle the tents of a Company, help to load
          the wagons,and unload,then set them up again,

Aug 4th, Very warm, No news from below, All quiet, good many yet on the
          sick list, Eighteen have died since the Regt left,

Aug 5th,   Hot as usual, Two men of Co "K buried to day,

Aug 6th, Morning some rain, cool this evening, wrote some letters,

Aug 10th, Past days with usual heat, My birth day 21 years old.
          All quiet. No news from the Regt,

Aug 11th, All the well men have gone to join the Regt at Natchez, Sick
           taken th the Hospilal, I am left alone,,One man to take care
           of the tents and camp equipage of the Company,

Aug 14th. Past two days about the same for heat, sultry and quiet, Corpl
          T N Lewis promoted to Sergt, T C Edland appointed Commissary
          Sergt, J F Roberts, appointed Corpl,

Aug 16th, Hot as usual, Nothing from the Regt. Great deal of sickness here,
          Many dying every day, Collored people dying rapidly.

Aug 18th,   Reported fighting at Natchez,

Aug 19th, Heavy rain last night, Fine breeze blowing and some cooler,
            Terrible accident, the Steamer City of Madison loaded with amunit-
            --tion , Blew up tearing the Boat all to pieces, Some forty or
            fifty soldiers and boatmen killed and wounded,The Steamer Ed
            Walsh lying near had her wheel torn off, Engineer killed, part
            of the cabin blown away, A negro woman was blown out in the
            river picked up by a tug ,unhurt, They were carring in fixed
            amunition,loading the Boat, Supposed some one dropped a box of
            percussion shell for field gun this exploded and the rest went w
            up at the same time,The explosion shook the town, I felt the jar
            way up in my tent a mile or so away,

Aug 2oth, Noon,rained all this morning, Quiet about camp,and town,

Aug 21st,   Orders at last to pack up and move, Only one colored man to help
            me, Took down the tents, loaded on wagons and hauled to the
            levee then: loaded aboard the Steamer White Cloud,Got about
            half done loading, When orders came to the Boatmen to go up the
            river, The 15th Iowa Inftry marched on board, The Steamer backed
            out and headed up the river and run nearly all night, reached
            Goodrichs landing 6o miles above Vicksburg,

Aug 22d,   Unloaded and on our way   down the river, Arrived at
            Vicksburg finished loading the Brigade camp equipage ,

Aug 23d,Started for Natchez, Passed Grand Gulf at sun down, And just as
            the moon went down reached Natchez, Boys delighted to see me
            and more especially to have the tents and mess chests, As they
            had been bivouacing all this time,

Aug 24th,   At work unloading the Boat, Got part of the tents up to camp.
            Sergt Edland came down to the Boat with a pony for me to ride
            Rode on through the city and to the camping place,Telling the
            Boys of my experience , sickness, moving camp, and what a time
            I had getting on the Boat the trip up the river and back then on
            down here, They telling me what a nice time they have had in
            the bovouac at Natchez,

Aug 25th, Finally hauled tents and equipage to the edge of town nice place
            for camp. pitched tents and taking it easy, grass shade,and water
            handy, Cool and quiet,

Aug 26th,   The usual drills and eveing parade, So many colored people
here and how they do dress, streets are ~~full~~ *alive with them* in the cool of the
evening,

Aug 27th,   Natchez is quite a nice City on the hill, the old part is called
Natchez under the hill. this is down next the river at the landin
Our camp is on the blue grass with fine shade trees,

Aug 28th,   Rather cool and pleasant, Wrote some letters, Privates
W J Green and J D Lyons appointed Corpls of Co "B,
Order of Lieut Dean Corpl Lyons placed in charge of a lot of
cotton in an old wagon yard right in the main part of town,

Aug 29th,   Every afternoon we have Battalion drill for about an hour. The Col
puts us through, Fall in on the Company parade ground, Then form on
the Regimental parade ground and march out in column of fours,
tn the drill ground an open space, Generally in our shirt sleeves,
most any way as it is hot. Of course we have our catridge boxes and
muskets, along with us as part of our equipments, The boys take a
good deal of interest in these drills, On one occasion I kept
repeating all the movements in mind, From column of fours to line,
From line to double column. From double column closed"en mass"
To column against cavalry, To form square, reduce square, Column
again back to line, Like to column of Companies by either flank to
column of fours and march back to camp, and dismiss,I went over it
in mind like the "House that Jack built", An hours drill,

Aug 30th, We have a delightful camping place here,,Shade and grass with
a slopeing parade ground in front, Sufficient to drain the
water off when it rains, Hot days and cool nights,

Aug 31st, On guard, Boys just coming in from Battalion drill.
Muster for pay at 9 A M,

Sept 1st, Relieved from guard duty at 7 A M. Quiet and cool. Boys on drill,
Company drill in the morning instead of marching generally
have manuel of arms in quarters,

Sept 2d,   Water melons gone, apples scarce, vegetables plenty. Pedlers
            in camp every day with pies, cakes, milk and vegetables,
            Asked little darkey boy how he sold pies,"ten cents 'piece
            fo' for dollar",

Sept 3d, Camp is kept clean and every thing in order, Our duty is light.
            The darkeys do the heft' of the work, We have roll call in the
            morning and Company drill before breakfast. Then at 8 A M,
            Battalion drill of about an hour some times two hours, After
            drills we can get passes for town. Five passes are given each
            day per Company. After dinner Company drill, and dress parade
            in the evening about 6 o'clock, Retreat, then taps at 9P M,
            lights out and to bed,

Sept 4th, The Regt is much stronger since the consolidation of the 109th,
            We call them the New boys",and the others the " Old boys",

Sept 5th, Detailed for picket, On the out post on Pine Ridge road, myself
            Corpl', and 10 men,In the woods there is a fine large wild grape
            called the "muscadine"they are very nice having a musky flavor.
            As they are plenty we have all we can eat, And we certainly
            enjoy them,

S ept 6th, Sunday morning, Relieved from picket, Returned to camp,
                Visited with Len Pierpont of the 76th Ills, They are camped
                near,

Sept 7th, Moved our camp this morning, As the line of fortifications that
            is being constructed goes right through our camping place The Company
            is now without Officers, Capt Vore is home on furlough. 1st
            Lieut S B Dean promoted Major of the 6th Miss' Colored Inftry.
            2d Lieut J D Vernay absent on detached service on Genl

        McPherson's staff, 2d Sergt Warren Peck promoted Capt Co "C 6th Miss
        Colored Inftry, Geo B Shaw 1st Sergt present and in comand of the
            Company,
        Sept 8th, On guard, Corpl of the Commissary guard, Privates Loony of Co "E
                Forage guard, Privates Henkle Co"E   ("   Lewis of Co "E,
                    "   Thomason " "B
                    "   Pate   " "B,   ("   Henry " " "E,
            Guards stand two huors and off four for the twenty four hours,
            Genl Mc Arthur was up to see the Regt on Parade this evening.

(134)

Forage guard, Privates, Hinkle of Co "B,   Guards stand two hours
      " " Thomason" """B,   and off four, for the
                                  twenty four hours,
      " " Pate " " B,

Genl Mc Arthur was up to see the Regt on Parade this evening,
Very warm,

Sept 9th,   76th Regt gone over the river on a scout,
Weather fine, duty light, but this isint putting down
the rebellion,

Sept 10th,   Boys returning from furlough, had a good time home, and
now glad to get back to the Regt, fresh and ready for
duty,

Sept 11th,   Usual camp duties, Boys will get over in town and come in
late, generally sober, not very much drinking, as it is
pretty hard for a soldier to get whiskey out side of the
commissary,

Sept 12th,   There is at the foot of the row of tents a small bridge
across a ditch, boys get on this bridge pat and dance
"juba", sing songs way late in the night, disturbs the
old fellows, hear e'm growl,

Sept 13th
      Battalion drill, sun shine, and dust,

Sept 14th   Went out on Battalion drill this morning, suddenly a
messenger rode up to the Col, spoke to him and departed,
Col flanked the Regt brought us into column of fours
double quick back to camp, ordered to get full equipments
and rations, fall in and marched to the Boat, quickly
on board, and off across the river to the Louisanna side,
debarked and marched out a mile or so, it seems the
Guerrillas attacked the Pontoon train men stationed on
this side, killed two, wounding several others, and ran
off with about 75 mules, and other plunder and made good
their escape, The 95th Ills, the 11th and some mounted
men   went after them but could not catch any of them,
at 5P M, layed down in a corn field and slept soundly all
night,

Sept 15th,   No disturbance through the night, no rebs in sight,
Some of the boys set fire to a house more for "devilment"
than revenge, the Col came riding furiously down and in
a very excited manner asked "Who set that house on fire",
Answer "Some of the boys in the left wing",

Galloping   to the left he again asked " Who set that house on fire,

"Some of the Boys of the right wing",   was the answer,

thats all any one knew about it and in the mean time the house

was burned down,3 P M returned to the Boat crossed over and
marched through town and on to camp, glad enough to get back,

Sept 16th,

Corpl of the Commissary Guard, Privates Barret of Co "B,
                                      "   Wells " " "A,
       Rations,fresh beef, salt pork, "   Barringer " "B,
       Beans, hard bread, sugar, salt,
       Coffee,soap and candles,

Sept 17th, Moved our camp out on the Kingston road, about a mile.

south of town,While drilling the manuel of arms just

before going on parade,this evening, we had the command to

fix bayonet, at the same time Co "E immediatly in our rear

had the command to " fire,which they did or at least one of

them did, the bullet passing through the tents, between me

and the man on my right, and struck Private S W, Cummings

who was in the front rank, the bullet passed through his thigh

cut the bayonet in two, broke the bone of his left fore arm
and lodged there,pieces of the bayonet out the side of my face,

He turned out of ranks and we closed up and marched out to the

line formed for parade, He was just in the act of drawing the

bayonet from the scabbard,when the shot occured, The Co "E

man had been on guard and neglected to discharge or draw the

bullet from his musket, had forgotton it was loaded,

when a bullet cuts a steel bayonet in two it surely has some

force, if it hadent' been that the bayonet stopped its flight
most likely to have killed some one in next Co,

Sept 18th, Went up town, saw Cummings in the City Hospital, he is doing

as well as could be expected,

Sept 19th,   We have a large box near the cook shanties, during the night

dark forms were seen coming in with aparrantly gunny sacks on
their shoulders, these were empted in the box with a thumping

sound, other wise the night was dark and quiet in camp,

Sept 20th,Sunday, quite a lot of sweet potatos in our box this morning,

they are very fine sliced and fried in grease,

(136)

Regimental Inspection at 8 oclock,an attack expected from some

forces out in the country, Heavy pickets sent out,8 P M, all

quiet,

Sept 21th, Morning pleasant and no rebels yet,

8 P M,Had some fine music from our Brigade Band,

Sept 22d,   Nothing of interest to day,

Sept 23d, Sergt Andrew Drake and Private Wm Morris, started &home
for
on furlough,this morning, Weather fine , cool nights,

Sept 24th, All quiet on the Missippippi,

Sept 25th, Weather warm and very dry, Obtained a pass, walked through

town, nothing of interest going on ,called on Cummings,He

is getting along fast, his wounds are doing well,
healing and doing
very well,

Sept 26th, Morning,cool and refreshing, some appearance of rain and

we need it bad enough, cisterns nearly dry, dust from

two to four inches deep in the roads, Our Brigade Band

gave us a serenade last night, Battalion drill at 7 oclock

this morning, that is if the Officers are up in,time.

Sept 27th,Sunday, Regimental Inspection by Major Mc Kee, we are short

of clothing but otherwise made a good appearance,
Several of our line Officers returned yesterday from
furloughs, Among them was Capt Vore of "B and his brother

I D Vore Wagon Master of the Regt, A lovely day, after

evening parade the mail came in I re'cd letters from home,
Some talk of the Pay WMaster coming soon,

Sept 28th,Quietly in camp , wrote letters home, Only two in my tent

the other two are on furlough,xxxxxx

Sept 29th,Rainy day, just enough fallen to lay the dust,was up town

saw Cummings he is doing well, 3 P M more rain,

Sept 30th,Detailed for guard at Genl Smith.sHead Quarters,our Brigade
Commander now,Ransom having left us into the Potomac Army,
gone
Rained all day,
Head Quarter Guard, Hughs of Co "F
"   "   " Murphy" " "B
"   "   " Still " " "K
"   "   "" Lents " " "H
"   "   " Cox   " " "I,
Carrington Corpl of the guard,

Oct 1st,

(137)

Oct 1st, Relieved from guard at 8 A M, Cleared off and at 2 P M, sun shining quite pleasantly, drying fast, spent the

day in cleaning arms and equipments,

Oct 2d, Morning quiet, 2 P M, Battallion Drill occupied an hour,

very interesting, the Companies march in pretty fair order and alinement,

Oct 3d, Corpl of the cistern guard,Privates Verble pf Co" B,
            " " JVerble " " E,
            " " Stewart " " E,

Weather fine, It is reported that Bragg and Rosecrans, have had a battle, result not known,at least not here,
                             noise
Brigadeer Genl Smith, Says that our Regt makes so much about

camp , and that chickens, sheep,turkeys, and hogs,have been
                          will
missing from the neighboring plantations,That he shall have to put on a camp guard, which will make our duty quite heavy,

A warning to all chicken stealers,I wonder if he thinks that,

will put a stop to it, I dont, In the first place he has to

prove it, and secondly he says he has not caught any of the

11th yet,"Bully for Brigadier Genl R, Smith,2d Brigade,1st

Division,"

Oct 4th, Relieved from guard this morning,Camp guard went on yesterday,

we are housed now, Rosecrans battle with Bragg confirmed, heavy loss on both sides, recd a letter from Vicksburg,

Oct 5th, On guard at Genl Quitmans place,we were treated very nice by

the occupants, while off duty part of the night curled up in

an old time silk lined coach for a few hours sleep, very likely

no soldier ever slept there before,

Oct 6th, Relieved this morning at 9 A M, and returned to camp,

Review at 4 P M, weather fine,all quiet about camp and town,

Oct 7th, Rained last night, wet and muddy this morning,Draw clothing,

Not well some thing like fever, not on the sick list,

Oct 8th, On picket at the out post on the Woodville road, Myself and

six men, Privates Wiggs of Co "C,
      " " Wealthy " " C,
      " " Weatherly " C,
      " " Jammie " C,
      " " Cadwhole per C,
      " " Cavins " C,
nothing transpired worth relating, light frost fell during

the night,

Oct 9th, Relieved at 1o A M, returned to camp, not very well to day,
          reported some cases of yellow fever in town,

Oct 1oth   All quiet, not very well,

Oct 11th, Down tents, pack up ready to leave camp at Natchez,

          Started at 1o3o A M, marched down to the river and aboard
          the Steamer Fort Wayne,all aboard left the landing at

          4 3o P M, steamed up the river 1o miles after wood,
          took on wood and tied up for the night,

Oct 12th,   Started about 5 oclock this morning, In company with the

          Fleet, five Boats in all, the E H. Fairchild is the Flag
          Ship, just before dark a heavy storm came upon us,blowed and

          rained for some time, all wet, about 1o P M, tied up for the
          night,

Oct 13th,Started early this morning and arrived at Vicksburg 1o A M,

          with out accidenty left the Boat, stacked arms and unloaded

          our traps,"then marched out about a mile from town and

          bivouacedfor the night,

Oct 14th,Awaiting all day to locate a place to camp, the tents arrived

          and finally we established our camp on the ground we

          occupied last night,

Oct 15th,   Pitched tents and moved our selves in , pleasant and cool,

Oct 16th, We are camped nearly in the old place wee were in before

          we left for Natchez,th e health of the city is much better

          since cool weather set in, Yellow fever is played out since

          the frosts, our duty will be heavy as we will have about
          seven miles of rifle pitts to picket, (the old rebel lines,)

          My tent faces the south is occupied by myself and two other
          a bunk on each side about two feet from the ground,

          canes laid on forks and poles, on these we spread our

          blankets and sleep very comfortable,the muskets stand up

          by the pole at back end, cat'ridge boxes, haversack and

          canteen with one or two towels hang from the top pole,

          candle stuck in a bayonet gives us"light on the subject!

Oct 17th, Cool and windy, Visited Fort Ransom, Our old camp and

          some of Logans works during the seige,some of the

                  ditches have been filled up and the Jackson road runs

          over them , Fort Hill has been rebuilt, but no guns

          mounted as yet, they are now building a heavy line of works

in side the old rebel works and much nearer town,The negros are
employed on the Forts,The 9th La Infty Colored, came in last night,

Oct 18th, Sunday pleasant and warm, quietly in camp,

Oct 19th, Detailed for picket , On post opposite our old position during
the Seige,Several of the boys while off duty are picking
up bullets, they sell the lead for 3 cents per pound,
pick up an old rotten gunny sack and shake out a handful of
bullets, we cut a narrow ditch in the clay soil, make a fire
melt the lead and let it run in the ditch thus making a bar,
that will weigh about two pounds or more, just back of Fort
Hill in a little ravine, where our shells burst during the seige
one can pick up a bushel of pieces of shell, the brass bands
around the butt of elongated shot is valuable, and much is
being gathered up and sold, abundance of iron,lead, and brass,
It must cost a large amount of money to fire away so much
old iron,brass,and lead,(I picked up 30# of lead,) mostly from
our intrenchments out side,

Oct 20th, Releved from picket and returned to camp,
Cool and cloudy appearance of rain,

Oct 21st,   The cuts along the Jackson road have door ways on the sides.
entrances dug out,then large rooms made and arched by the
ones that made them, here the citizens spent the nights safe from
bullets and shells,the clay is of such a nature that it stands
a long time just as it was cut,a name carved on the side of the
road remains there, our bullets were more dangerous than the big
shells,
bullets singing down that road hit and killed and wounded a great
many, while the shells could be seen coming so they could hunt their
holes, nights were the most dreary and dismal,full of danger,
the dread and fear were heart rending, I saw where 1 inch shells
had burst in dwelling houses, tearing out partitions, knocking down
plaster and fairly wrecking the house, some burst five or six
feet in the ground, many burst in the air, pieces weighting 50 or
more pounds falling a hundred feet would strike the ground hard,
Woe be to any one that was struck by these jagged pieces of iron
hot from the Mortar,

Oct 22d, Moved our camp about two miles south of our present location, wood handy, but water scarce, there is a pond near where we can wash, we generally depend upon springs for our water supply

Oct 23d Rainy day, All wet,and the boys housed up in the tents Another Steamer reported burned on the Mississippi , with camp and garris -on equipage sufficient for several Regts,This burning of Uncle Sams Boats must be stopped,

Oct 24th, Pleasant and some warmer than yesterday, Signed the pay rolls, have now four months pay due,

Oct 25th,Detailed to work on the breast works, this being sunday we were dismissed, Cool morning white frost last night,

Oct 26th, Arranging our camp as is most likely will winter here, We dig out a square hole about the size of the tent, some three or four feet deep, set the tent over this and peg it down securely, ditch around on the out side,cut steps in front to get down into the basement,at the back side we cut out a fire place, then two or three barrels on top for chimney, plaster these up with mud, and we have a nice comfortable fire in the tent,our bunks made of forks and poles or canes on each side accomodate four men, A soldier can be home like in camp if he will work a little.

Oct 27th, At work cleaning up grounds for parade and drill.other wise quiet about camp and town,

Oct 28th, Drake and others returned from furlough, had a good time at home and now ready for camp and duty,

Oct 29th, All quiet about camp,

Oct 30th, Weather pleasant,

Oct 31st, Mustered for pay at 9 A M,

Nov 1st, Sunday morning, cloudy,Nothing of interest going on,

Nov 2d, &3d, Good deal of a sameness in camp,

Nov 4th, Detailed for work on the intrenchments, all day, weather warm, In digging these ditches we often come across corn stalks and other trash some six or eight feet below the surface washed in by the rains, we find these pitts are made by the big shells

(141)

being driven in the ground and exploding make these holes, the

pieces are found dpressed against the sides, this accounts for

the"muffled roar" we noticed during the seige,The breast work is
four feet thick on top abuat 12 to15 ft at the bottom, the ditch is
8 ft deep and 8 to 1o ft wide, strong forts on high ground for heavy
guns,
Nov 5 th Wet and damp this mornong, rain last night,Some talk of our

being payed this week, The rest of the Brigade has been paid

two months pay,   The old 2oth Ills has reenaisted to aman,
There is grit in that little old Regt, They number only about
7o or 8o men for duty, but they are now"veterans! Our Regt
is now about six to 8oo strong, There is some expeaition on

foot as they are fitting up a train of 12o wagons for the 17th

  Army   Corps,   Genl Mc Pherson commanding.

Nov 6th, Morning pleasant, Payed off, received $56,1o,

gained some on my clothing account,

Furloughs made out for three men in Co "B, Powers, Cummings and (

Carrington,

Nov 7th,   Morning clear, Boys are doing a little business on their own
hook,buy a barrel of oranges and sell them out,

Nov 8th, Sunday, Regimental inspection at 1o A M,by Col James H Coats,

of the 11th Ills Inftry,Afternoon fine,

Nov 9th,
        Furloughs suspended by order of Genl Mc Pherson, weather fine.
    I am disapointed, was all ready to start for home with $45, in
    my pocket,
Nov 1oth,   Boys playing seven up and chuck luck,must have some thing
               to keep up some little excitement, so they get interested
        in these games, some times we have jumping matches, run rases
       get a 24 and 32 pound shot and see how far we can throw it,
Nov 11th,   Regimental inspection at 2 P M, One of Co "H men buried.

Corpl Warbus left for Ills, to recruit for the Company.

Private Cummings gone home on furlough, h is arm unfits

him for duty,

Nov 12th 13th
14th and 15th, Past few days about the same, weather warm with cool

            nights,some frost,
    Sunday, pleasant and warm, 3 P M, Brigade parade the 95thIlls,

            14th and 17th Wis, and the 11th Ills form the 2d Brigade,

Nov 16th,Cold this morning a fire is quite comfortable, boys are attending

the theatre in town pretty regular, $1oo per night isn't

much to a soldier,

Nov 17th
        All quiet in camp,

Nov 18th, Signed the pay rolls, J Brown died one of the new Boys,
L Pierpont came over to see me, his Brigade is up from
Natchez,

Nov 19th, All quiet, several cases of small pox in camp, one sent to
Hospital from our Co, others immediatly occupied the tent as
we are short of tents,

Nov 20th, Cold and raining, wind from the west, going to turn cold,

Nov 21st, Detailed for picket, Regt payed off,two months pay, I recd'
$26, weather pleasant,

Nov 22d, Sunday, Relieved from picket at 9 A M,returned to camp,
Regimental inspection this morning,No news, all quiet about
camp, warm ahd fine all day,

Nov 25th, Past few days same as usual with drills and camp duty &c&c,

Nov 26th, 2d Brigade of Crockers Division marches at 7 A M,tomorrow,

Some talk of our going to Chattanooga, (I hope so), all
quiet here, Thanksgiving Day no drill,

Nov 27th,
All quiet about camp, weather cool,

Nov 29th, Sunday, morning cold, Regimental inspection by Col Coates,

Nov 30th, Morning pleasant but cold, ground frozen,there is a pond
near where we go mornings to wash our faces, some ice
on the pond this morning,
Co drill at 10 A M, Battalion drill at 2 P M,Corpl George D,
Carrington appointed Sergt, Privates John Brown, and Alex
Powers appointed Corpls in Co "B,(sent home $15)

Dec 1st, Warmer this morning, Powers,(Calamity) as we call him,
has been in the habit of calling a Corpl,"A two stripe hound"
now after his promotion we torment him, by calling him"A two
striped hound", he is a splendid shot,and we know about how
far we can tease him and get away safely,

Dec 2d,
Weather is fine again, On fatugue duty, cleaning up around
Camp, Latest news , Bragg badly whipped by Grant near Chatt-
-a nooga,

Dec 3d, Some times during the night, some of the Boys have been
quite lively around camp, and making themselves most too
conspicuous,by throwing ca'tridges down the barrel chimneys
into the fire places, and make a very unpleasant explosion,

(142)B

Nov 30th,

Small pox in camp. many vaccinated and as result have very sore
arms,
My arm was swollen and sore could not handle musket so excused
from duty for several days,

More men sick from the vaccination that from the small pox.
We care nothing about small pox. as fast as men leave for the
Hospital others take posession of their tents as we are short of
tents.All so far get well anyhow.

(143)

Dec 4th, & 5th, Appearance of rain,

Dec 6th, Sunday, pleasant, Inspection of arms, quarters,and equipments, same as usual,

The boys were running quite a line of "chuck luck" banks on south side of the line of tents, The Col came along,and? Boys put these things up fxxxxxxxxxx and observe the day quietly, while I am not a very religous man my self,still I can't approve of this on sunday," every man to his tent",

Dec 7th, A review takes place tomorrow if the weather permits, Capt Vore offeres $5, to the man that has the cleanest gun and equipments,

Dec 8th, Rained last night, Review comes off at 12 30 P M,To much mud think it will be postponed,

Dec 9th, Had our inspection,and private John Stamps got the $5, for the cleanest musket in the Co, Mine was next and the First Sergt Shaw gave me $2, I noticed after parade last evening that Stamps was wipeing and cleaning his musket before putting it up , I had looked over mine also to see it was in good condition, after the inspection the Capt couldent decide between us, so he sent for the Col, He inspected both piesse carfully, when he took mine,and drew the rammer and sprang it in the barre; then took out from his pocket a white handkerchief and wiped the head of the rammer, I thought I was done for then,but he found no marks on the handkerchief, however as he returned the rammer he noticed dust in the pipe, that settled it,I had overlooked that, so John beat me, It was all good natured, no hard feelings I awlways prided myself on a clean bright musket and bayonet, as well as all my equipments,

Dec 10th, Appearance of rain, the 95th Ills have inspection and review to day,

Dec 11th,& 12th, Damp and rainy weather, all quiet,

Dec 13th, Warmer, Some talk of our leaving Vicksburg,

Dec 18th, Cold but pleasant this morning, been wet with thunder in the past few days, dismal, gloomy weather,It all depends on the weather how we fare in camp, while we are warm enough in our tents the mud is disagreeable,

Dec 4th,

Several of the Boys wanted to be teamsters, A detail is made for that
purpose, The man goes to the Corral and selects two large mules for the
tongue, Two smaller mules for the swing,and two yet smaller for lead,
Choosing also the color whether bay, brown, black or grey,These mules are
all wild never been under harness,So with a man,and some times several to
help,they catch two and chain them to a fence, tree, or the wheels of the
large Government wagon,bring out four more to make the team of six mules.
Then after a desperate battle put the harness on and buckle it up tight,
Now they hitch them to the wagon.This requires a good deal of time and
patience as well as some "curs" words, They chain each wheel, Five or six
men get in the wagon, The driver now mounts the saddle mule which is the
near" mule on the tongue, He has just one line hitched to the near lead
mules'bit, and a black snake whip, Now the fun begins , The driver cracks
his whip, jerks the line and shouts "getap" they start or try to,then the
lead mules turn short around and start back towards the wagon, A few cracks
of the " black snake" in their faces turn them back.Then they try the other
side, A right hand lick on the off mules rump then a crack or two at the
swing team and they start to run but the wagon holds them down, They soon
get to pulling, In a few days have a team broke and at work.
Generally takes two or three men to hitch them up a few times then the
driver and his helper can manage all right,On the road and march as they
near the camping place the mules always begin to bray,

(144)

Dec 19th, Sunday warm and pleasant,   One of Co "K men buried to day,

Regimental inspection at 10 A M, all quiet and no news,

Dec 20th,   Much talk about erenlisting as"veterans"for three more years,

a bounty of $300, is offered, quite an inducement especially

as we expect to stay any how and see the war through,

that is some of us, others will go home when their term of
enlistment expires,

Dec 21st,   Enlisted for three years if not sooner discharged, In the

"Veteran Volunteers,"

Dec 22d, & 23d, It was between Drake and Myself who should go on picket,

Sergt Shaw called on me, but I insisted it was Drakes turn,

so we ate breakfast and kept on eating thinking the one that

was longest at the table would be the one to stay, finally the

Drum beat and Drake threw up ,grabbed his musket and equipment

and was off as Sergt of the Picket post,
            Shaw
Sergt afterwards told me Drake had been excused, so really it

was my turn,(the only time I ever refused duty,)

Dec 24th, Weather pleasant and warm, Boys having lots of fun,Each Co

made their Capt treat to the apples , Mustered in for three

years, 'Veterans",We take a great deal of pride in the fact we

are"Veterans,"

Dec 25th, Every thing closed up in town, Streets full of soldiers,

some drinking, our Boys off to town, quiet in camp,

Dec 26th,   Quiet,after the Christmas rejoicing,

Dec 27th, Sunday, Rained last night, wet and muddy to day,

Making out furloughs for the Veterans , five in number in

our Co,

Dec28th, On picket duty, cool,

e 29th, Relieved from picket at 9 A M, all quiet in camp.

Two more of Co B" reenlisted for three years making seven "

all,

30th, Rained all day,

st, Rained all last night and still at it this morning,
Muster for pay if the weather permits. End of 1863.

www.ingramcontent.com/pod-product-compliance
Lightning Source LLC
Chambersburg PA
CBHW081135090426
42740CB00014BA/2874